PRISON SENTENCES:

THE PRISON AS SITE/THE PRISON AS SUBJECT

organized by:
Julie Courtney and Todd Gilens

works by:
Beth B
Jonathan Borofsky
James Casebere
Malcolm Cochran
Willie Cole
with the Fabric Workshop
Simon Grennan & Christopher Sperandio
Carolyn Healy and John Phillips
Homer Jackson and Mogauwane Mahloele
with John Abner, Richard Jordan and
Lloyd Lawrence
Christina Kubisch
Winifred Lutz
Virgil Marti
Bruce Pollock
Fiona Templeton
with Amnesty International
Allan Wexler

Project Directors: Julie Courtney and Todd Gilens

Educational Outreach: Jenni Desnouee and Ann Karlen

Administrative Assistants: Lisa Basil, Jennifer Biancaniello, and Halima McMullen

Installation Supervisor: Jennie Shanker

Site Manager: Sean Kelley

Site Monitors and Guides: Sophie Brookover, Clem Coleman, Paul Eisenhauer, Tanya Fischer, Melissa Heller, Ann Howland, Jon Manteau, Erik Nabors, Elizabeth Noznesky, Annelise Ream, Heather Skowood, Jeff Smith, and Shira Walinsky.

Photographs of the artwork were taken by Jack Ramsdale unless otherwise noted.
Cover Photo by Barry Halkin
Inside Back Cover Photo by Todd Gilens

Catalogue Designed by Assemblage Inc., Phila.
Printed and bound in the United States of America

ISBN 0-9649221-1-8
Library of Congress Catalogue Card #95-071281

Available through D.A.P./Distributed Art Publishers
636 Broadway, 12th Floor, New York, NY 10012
Tel: 212.473.5119   Fax: 212.673.2887

© 1995 Moore College of Art and Design
The Parkway at 20th Street
Philadelphia, PA 19103

TABLE OF CONTENTS

PREFACE

Todd Gilens and Julie Courtney

"BY ASKING QUESTIONS THAT WOULD REVEAL ITS BURIED LAYERS OF MEANING, THE ARTWORKS CHALLENGE THE CONVENTIONS OF HISTORICAL PRESENTATION AND ANALYSIS."

a few days before the opening of *Prison Sentences*, Christina Kubisch was taking a break from adjusting her installation "Skylights," a series of cells lit only by black light and saturated with the eerie sounds of a glass armonica. After returning to her cellblock from a walk through "Why Malcolm had to Read," a cacophonous bacchanalia of images by Homer Jackson and his collaborators, an installation that is at once horrible, humorous, and incisive, she remarked: "We all are looking at the same place and making what we see there, but it comes out so differently!"

Historic sites are familiar to most of us, with their rangers and plaques, re-enactments and displays. In bringing site-specific artworks to Eastern State Penitentiary, we are using an unusual strategy to present this historic site. By asking questions that would reveal its buried layers of meaning, the artworks challenge the conventions of historical presentation and analysis. How are objects, places, and stories imbued with history? What is the relationship between imagination, human experience, and the objective world? Can history be properly expressed through the idioms of contemporary art? Our working hypothesis for this project is that artworks make connections that are both objectively valid and emotionally resonant. But in an atmosphere so emotionally charged and visually seductive, we sometimes wondered how the artworks would keep from being dwarfed, physically, intellectually, and morally. Would the artists' individual gestures be lost in the vast collectivity that Eastern State embodies?

The penitentiary's structure, scale, and textures presented an opportunity to challenge the conventions of display, but also posed their own difficulties. Artists had to contend with a continual seeping of water, plaster dust, and plant roots down through the cells. The labyrinth of corridors allows no simple route for visitors to follow; there are dead ends, branching halls, and false walls. Visitors are often on their own to decide where the artworks begin and end.

People sometimes come to Eastern State only to satisfy a curiosity inspired by its massive stone wall. But once inside, there is so much to do that we began to sell season passes for those who wanted to come back several times. There are five acres of corridors and yards through which visitors can discover and explore the artworks on their own, hourly tours that focus on the history of the site, daily tours of the exhibition, and a visitor center filled with historic artifacts to examine, videos to watch, and souvenirs and books to buy. The penitentiary has a strange magnetism, and we knew in advance that visitors would come to the prison from across the social spectrum, and that they would see what had been done at the site from within their own varied frames of reference. It was an extraordinary opportunity to share challenging contemporary artworks with a broad audience. We trusted the artists, as they embedded their works in a fascinating building, to communicate across these social boundaries.

Today's exploding prison populations and increasingly repressive approaches to crime call on us to learn more about what is really going on in the criminal justice system. Much can be learned from Eastern State about the meaning and nature of prisons, their "feel," and the development of their ideologies. We are very lucky to have access to this extraordinary site. But there is

4

a crucial gap between Eastern State today and functioning prisons, and that is the presence of prisoners. Prison is, among many other things, a battle waged over authority and autonomy. Inmates no longer choose for themselves when to bathe, when or what to eat, when to shut the light off at night; numbers are appended to their names, and their connections to community and to familiar places are regulated by someone else's rules.

In this abandoned penitentiary, itself struggling to maintain or transform its identity, we hope our exhibition points to that realm—the experience of the incarcerated—and to its many variants throughout society. But *Prison Sentences* is also a celebration of the freedom and ability to speak about the world as we see it, an affirmation of the validity and necessity of personal or communal vision. Christina Kubisch's remark about the differences in the installations speaks precisely to this point. It also indicates part of the reason for the failure of Eastern's famous program of isolation: reform cannot be programmatic unless there is an accounting for the vast and subtle range of individual differences. It is interesting to note in this context that the National Endowment for the Arts, a symbol of a national will to acknowledge the value of personal expression, awarded us our first major grant. The precariousness of the National Endowment is unnerving and disappointing, but far from surprising in the present atmosphere of politicized, retributive justice, and the mushrooming costs of prisons.

An exhibition of this kind requires the shared vision of literally hundreds of people. Having nurtured *Prison Sentences* over the last six years, it is enormously gratifying

Photo by James Casebere

to finally see the exhibition happen. There are many we would like to thank for their encouragement and support along the way. Dr. Richard Tyler of the Philadelphia Historical Commission guided us through our negotiations with the City of Philadelphia for permission to use Eastern State, making the experience almost enjoyable. Bill Bolger of the National Parks Service exceeded even our own enthusiasm for the inclusion of cultural programs at Eastern State and worked tirelessly beside us preparing the site for visitors. Milton Marks, of the Preservation Coalition of Greater Philadelphia, let us and hundreds of artists into the prison countless times in all sorts of weather and never grumbled about it. Barbara Price and Joe Dutka of Moore College of Art and Design

5

inherited the project when they joined the staff of Moore; nonetheless, they graciously hosted *Prison Sentences* and should rightfully share the pride in its success. Sally Elk first introduced us to Eastern State, and we are indebted to her for the opportunity. Our Advisory Board members, Penny Bach, Cee Brown, Pat Finio, John Higgins, Thora Jacobson, Mary Kilroy, Paula Marincola, Mark Rosenthal, Judy Stein, Richard Torchia, and Ella King Torrey, provided us with a wide range of support; they offered advice we didn't even know we needed.

We are grateful for other organizations around Philadelphia who shared our sense of urgency about these issues and who, in concert with *Prison Sentences* produced a wide variety of exhibitions, expanding access to artists working with prison issues. They are: Borders Bookshop, The Fabric Workshop/Museum, High Wire Gallery, The Galleries at Moore, the Painted Bride Art Center, The Philadelphia Art Alliance, The Education Corridor at the Philadelphia Museum of Art, The Rosenbach Museum & Library, Rosenwald-Wolf Gallery at The University of the Arts, The Tyler Galleries, Vox Populi, and The White Dog Cafe.

A number of organizations and individuals provided essential support to the artists. Amnesty International helped with research and gave tireless hands-on assistance to Fiona Templeton for "Cells of Release;" The Fabric Workshop/Museum aided Willie Cole with research and installation of "5 to 10;" and a fearless and talented installation crew secured doors and skylights, filled holes, replaced glass, and repaired ceilings to bring a ruined building to within the realm of public safety. Finally, the monitors, tour guides, and staff at

Eastern State have done an outstanding job presenting the site to the public and keeping the installations running.

We would also like to extend a very special thanks to the members of the Eastern State Penitentiary Task Force, whose enthusiasm, brilliance, humor, and hard work have laid the foundation for the preservation of Eastern State, and to the National Parks Service, the Pennsylvania Prison Society, and the Preservation Coalition of Greater Philadelphia, for their farsightedness, courage, and sensitivity in standing behind the redevelopment of Eastern State as an educational museum. We are indebted to our essayists Russ Immarigeon, Lucy Lippard, and Eileen Neff, for sharing their wealth through their writing. Designers Keith Ragone and Dave Adams produced unique publications throughout the exhibition and we are grateful for their talented energy.

There is no way to adequately thank the artists. We are truly grateful for their hard work and fertile imaginations, their generosity and their resolve in difficult circumstances. There would have been no exhibition without them.

Julie Courtney is an independent curator who lives in Philadelphia. She was the founding director of the Temple Gallery, and a consulting curator at the Institute of Contemporary Art in Philadelphia.

Todd Gilens is a Philadelphia-based sculptor and theater designer. The objects and environments he has created for performance have been seen throughout the United States.

Photo by James Casebere

7

Eastern State Penitentiary: From Closure to "Prison Sentences"

Richard Tyler

On October 25, 1829, Charles Williams, an eighteen-year old African American convicted of burglary by the Delaware County Court of Oyer and Terminer, entered Eastern State Penitentiary as its first inmate. Almost 141 years later, on April 14, 1970, the last twenty-eight prisoners passed through the gate of John Haviland's Gothic castle-like Administration Building on Fairmount Avenue to complete their sentences at Graterford.[1]

At Cherry Hill, an orchard in the outskirts of Philadelphia, well-meaning humanitarians of the early nineteenth century sought to address the perennial problem of deviant or asocial behavior with a penal system of solitary confinement realized in the stone and mortar of Eastern State Penitentiary. Associated with or inspired by the Philadelphia Society for Alleviating the Miseries of Public Prisons, now the Pennsylvania Prison Society, they thought that separateness would prevent moral contagion and would foster personal reformation through reflection and penitence. Haviland gave architectural expression to

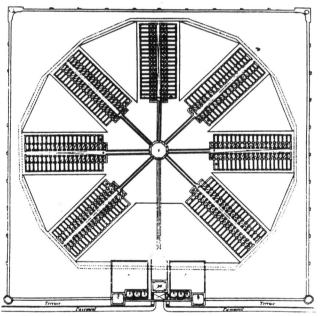

After John Haviland,
Plan of Eastern State Penitentiary,
c. 1829.

this concept with seven cellblocks, eventually increased to fourteen, radiating from a central rotunda and observation tower. For decades, penologists debated the comparative efficacy of Eastern State's solitary system and New York's Auburn system of isolation at night, silent congregate labor during the day, and corporal punishment to assure obedience. Cherry Hill, as the prison came to be known, also drew much attention from Americans and foreigners, including Charles Dickens, Gustave de Beaumont and Alexis de Tocqueville, and served as a model for over 300 prisons in other countries and states well into the present century. Although an improvement over the appalling Walnut Street Gaol, Eastern State Penitentiary, a "crucible of good intentions," failed. Charles Dickens, perhaps deceived by his frequently cited "dejected, heart-broken, wretched" German larcener cum weaver, did not stray far from the mark in finding Eastern State "a most dreadful, fearful place."[2]

The history of Eastern State Penitentiary did not end on April 14, 1970.[3] Less than three months after Eastern State's closure as a penitentiary, the Commonwealth of Pennsylvania and the City of Philadelphia entered a lease agreement that permitted the City to use Cherry Hill as a detention center. Within a few days, a violent riot at Holmesburg, a City prison and one of the numerous progeny of Eastern State, led to the temporary transfer of inmates to Cherry Hill. They, along with others from Holmesburg and persons awaiting trial, occupied Eastern State until moved else-where the next year.

At last, in 1971, Cherry Hill ceased to serve as a place of incarceration, and became a place for the storage of trucks, abandoned automobiles, equipment and supplies, and home for numerous cats. It also suffered from vandalism and a lack of maintenance. An era of decay, planning and reuse studies began.

In 1974, Mayor Frank L. Rizzo advocated razing Cherry Hill to make room for a criminal justice center. That scheme collapsed in the face of opposition from the adjacent neighborhoods and from the bench and bar. At the same time, the City Planning Commission looked to Eastern State for re-use as a bicentennial youth hostel or a museum of penology. The Commission also considered its potential as a cleared development site for an industrial park, a shopping center or housing. Yet other officials continued to hold onto the notion of a holding prison. During these early years of virtual abandonment and increasing deterioration, the preservation of the Penitentiary for its historical and architectural significance received scant notice, despite its listing as a National Historic Landmark in 1965.

In 1977, the City took title to Cherry Hill. Simultaneous residential reinvestment and rehabilitation in the immediate area stimulated further public and private interest in the site. The Planning Commission recommended a supermarket and housing with, once again, extensive if not total demolition. The incentives for historic preservation provided in the Economic Recovery Tax Act of 1981, however, caused both the City and the private sector to look to the adaptive re-use of the existing complex and its buildings. In pursuit of this opportunity, the City transferred Eastern State to the Redevelopment Authority for marketing in 1984. The Authority issued a

development package for residential re-use with controls that presumably would conform to the Secretary of the Interior's *Standards for Rehabilitation,* a prerequisite for the tax benefits. These included the preservation of the perimeter walls and of Haviland's original seven cellblocks.

Only one developer, John Rahenkamp and Associates, responded. They proposed the creation of 250 market-rate apartments in nine of the radial structures by dividing each of the cellblocks vertically. This scheme obviously would have compromised the integrity and uniqueness of the Haviland plan of individual cells on long double-loaded corridors, the defining element not only of the historic architectural significance of Eastern State Penitentiary but also of its austere and awesome aesthetic. An expensive undertaking, this re-use of Cherry Hill proved financially infeasible, because it necessitated a public subsidy of $30,000 per unit of market-rate housing. The City neither could have nor should have supplied these funds. Although thwarted by economics, Rahenkamp's plan did yield a recognition of the potential compatibility of preservation and development. Perhaps more importantly, it enhanced the awareness of Eastern State Penitentiary as more than the familiar and forbidding Administration Building and the high, thick walls.

In 1986, the Redevelopment Authority again advertised Eastern State. In this round, it solicited a commercial, residential or mixed use development, and attempted to make the property more attractive by markedly reducing the historic preservation criteria. It mandated only the retention of the perimeter walls and allowed penetration of them at two locations. Preservation of the

"THROUGH ART AND ARTISTS, THEY OFFER TO A YET BROADER AUDIENCE ANOTHER SET OF INTERPRETATIONS AND A NEW PERSPECTIVE FOR THE PENITENTIARY."

historic plan and buildings became only "a positive factor in the evaluation of proposals," not a *sine qua non* for the selection of a developer.[4] The experience of 1984 and economics seem to have dictated this decision. The site simply possessed greater monetary worth as cleared land than as an historic artifact densely filled with buildings perceived to have limited purposes. These same economics, however, contributed to the preservation of the walls, for the cost of demolishing them would doubtlessly have far exceeded the value of the land they occupied.

The Authority received four proposals in the spring of 1987 and forwarded them for review to the Philadelphia Historical Commission, the City's historic preservation agency. The Commission found the plans

wanting, for all four entailed extensive demolition. That fall, three of the four applicants made revised submissions with gestures toward the Commission's concerns. KODE Development Associates intended to retain the Administration Building, radically modify five of Haviland's seven cellblocks and the central rotunda for conversion into shops and offices, and to erect a supermarket surmounted by a parking garage in the northeast quadrant of the complex. Breslin Realty Development Corporation offered to keep the Administration Building, the gutted building envelope of two original cellblocks and the observation tower, and to construct a 50,000 square foot supermarket with parking. Historical Developers of Pennsylvania planned to preserve only the Administration Building, Cellblock Four and the rotunda. A plaza, stores, apartments and a parking garage would occupy the balance of the site. Little sense of Haviland' design would have survived the implementation of any of these proposals.

As the developer selection process moved with seeming inexorability, opposition to the loss or mutilation of Eastern State mounted among the public and in the press. Neighborhood people, historians, academics, architects, planners and curators coalesced in the Eastern State Penitentiary Task Force, which later became a committee of the Preservation Coalition of Greater Philadelphia. The Authority set April 29, 1988 as the date to name a developer. In response to the concerns of the Task Force and others, however, Mayor W. Wilson Goode took up the issue with his planning and development advisers during the morning of April 27; that afternoon he met with members of the Task Force. Two days later, he urged the Redevelopment Authority to exercise its option of rejecting all the proposals for Eastern State.

Mayor Goode committed the City to work with the preservation community through the Historical Commission to devise a solution for Cherry Hill. Since then, the City and the Coalition Task Force have had a series of studies completed, including a condition assessment analysis, a protection and stabilization plan, an historic structures report, and a marketing and interpretive program. The administration of Mayor Edward G. Rendell has continued this effort and is now prepared to seek proposals from concessionaires for the management and operation of Eastern State Penitentiary as an historic site. In addition, under license from the City, the Coalition Task Force and the Prison Society have conducted an expanding and encouraging tour program that attracted some 12,000 visitors to Eastern State during the summer of 1994.

In a sense, *Prison Sentences: The Prison as Site/The Prison as Subject* constitutes an extension of the activities of the Coalition Task Force and the Prison Society. It, too, seeks to foster the awareness, understanding and perception of Cherry Hill as a significant historic artifact and as a cultural asset. Attracted by Eastern State's extraordinary aesthetic, exhibition organizers Julie Courtney

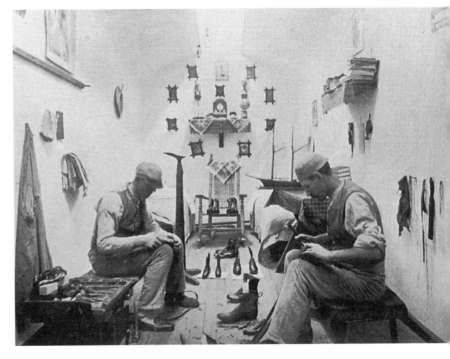

Shoemaking in a cell at Eastern State, late 19th century. *State Prisons, Hospitals, Soldiers Homes and Orphan Schools controlled by the Commonwealth of Pennsylvania,* From Amos H. Mylin, 2 vols. (n.p. 1879)

and Todd Gilens employ a different lens—art. Through art and artists, they offer to a yet broader audience another set of interpretations and a new perspective for the Penitentiary.

With subtlety, whimsy, pathos, isolation, rage, irony and conscience, *Prison Sentences,* however, transcends the Penitentiary as artifact. It evokes and, indeed, forces reflection on the still unresolved problems and failures that brought the Prison Society into existence, Charles Williams behind these walls, and Eastern State Penitentiary into being as concept and site.

Dr. Richard Tyler has been director of the Philadelphia Historical Commission since 1974.

1 For a recently published full account of Eastern State Penitentiary, see Norman Johnston with Kenneth Finkel and Jeffrey A. Cohen, *Eastern State Penitentiary: Crucible of Good Intentions* (Philadelphia, 1994). See also Marianna Thomas Architects, *Eastern State Penitentiary: Historic Structures Report* (3 vols., 1994) (on file with the Philadelphia Historical Commission).

2 Charles Dickens, *American Notes* (New York, n.d.), p. 111; Letter from Charles Dickens to John Forster, in Johnston, *Eastern State Penitentiary,* p. 57, citing Philip Collins, *Dickens and Crime* (London, 1962), p. 120.

3 For a fuller account of Eastern State Penitentiary since 1970, see Dennis R. Montagna, *Philadelphia's Eastern State Penitentiary: These Stone Walls Do Not a Shopping Center Make,* in Linda H. Schneekloth, Marcia R. Feuerstein and Barbara A. Compagna, ed., *Changing Places: Remaking Institutional Buildings* (Freedonia, N.Y., 1992), pp. 258-280. The files of the Philadelphia Historical Commission contain extensive materials on the development and planning activities of the post-closure period.

4 Redevelopment Authority of Philadelphia, *Redevelopment Controls for Former Eastern State Penitentiary,* 1986 (on file with the Philadelphia Historical Commission).

THE ROAD TO HELL [1]

Lucy R. Lippard

When the search for the new is applied to the old, local history explodes into possibilities. The tangle of memories residing in Everyplace is fluid and changing and open to as many interpretations as the market will bear, although the feeling of reverence sought by monument-makers is not easy to come by in an irreverent society. When the site of recall is a penitentiary, the shadow side prevails: hints of violence, passion, greed, of lives lost and left behind bars. The structure is inextricable from the events that landed people there and the social contexts in which they took place. One urban site radiates to others, and the parts can help define the whole.

A local public is rarely conscious of the communally shared meanings inherent in urban spatial history. One reason to understand what is "around here" is to ensure that we are not defined by others, so that we can resist other people's images of *our* pasts. Most historical preservation projects commodify "heritage" while claiming to replicate "what it was like back then," how "they" were like us and not like us, and what that means to us. Because of our social ease with simulacra, Americans are probably more drawn to a created image than to any accurate rendition of other times and their places, with the bad smells and offensive sights. To bring people closer to lived experience, a provocative community exercise would be to ask people what local existing sites/buildings/artifacts they would like to see saved for posterity and how; what disappeared histories they would like to see resurrected and why. I wonder if prisons would even be on the list.

In his 1972 book *What Time is This Place?* [3] (which presciently laid out most of the arguments about history and authenticity extended today), Kevin Lynch wrote that the preservation of a certain kind of past channels us into a certain kind of future. He asked the core questions about historical preservation: Why save things and what should be saved? Which era of a place's long life should be chosen as a focus? Among Lynch's other questions, which should be asked of any landmark site are:

Are we looking for evidence of the climactic moments or for any manifestation of tradition we can find, or are we judging and evaluating the past, choosing the more significant over the less, retaining what we think of as best? ...Should things be saved because ...they are unique or nearly so or ...because they were most typical of their time? Because of their importance as a group symbol? Because of their intrinsic qualities in the present? Because of their special usefulness as sources of intellectual information about the past? Or should we (as we most often do) let chance select for us and preserve for a second century everything that has happened to survive the first? ...To what degree does contemporary utility, however discreetly provided, rupture the sense of historical integrity?

These questions are the basis of a dialogue in which artists' voices should be heard. Historic sites can be seen not as closures, but as social catalysts. What is largely absent in the dialog is an exploration of the process of cultural construction, an exposure of the choices that have been made and the bases for interpretation, and interconnections between contemporary society and the site in its present state. J.B. Jackson says that we perceive history "not as a continuity but as a dramatic discontinuity, a kind of cosmic drama." [4] The museological notion that the antique object maintains importance even if we no longer

"A CULTURE CANNOT BE REDUCED TO AN ARTIFACT AS LONG AS IT IS BEING LIVED."

Raymond Williams [2]

A correct view of the State Prison,

IN THE VICINITY OF PHILADELPHIA.

The above represents a front view of the form of the new Penitentiary now building near this city.

This spacious edifice was planned by Mr. John Haviland, under whose superintendence the work is going on. When completed, it will constitute, it is believed, one of the most efficient, and withal, most merciful corrections of vice, that has ever been built. We design giving some general idea of its interior structure, together with the mode of treatment, to which its unhappy inmates, for crime, will be subjected. The object of the architect has been, to plan a building, in which a very large number of convicts might be confined, subject to suitable labor, and with the least possible intercourse with their fellow criminals, and even with the persons appointed to oversee their labor and superintend their cells.—That this object has been effected in an eminent degree, it would seem evident from examination of the structure; nor has the important consideration of the prisoners comfort been overlooked—light, heat and cleanliness, are provided for. The following gives some idea of the structure of the cells and their interior economy:—

"The seven blocks of cells which form the body of the design, are of the most simple form, being parallellograms, which, by their disposition, possess all the advantages of a polygeon figure without the expense attending it. Each building contains 36 cells, (twelve feet long, eight feet wide, and ten feet high, with an exercising yard to each. The partition walls between the cells are calculated to be 18 inches in thickness, and their foundation three feet deep: the wall next the passage is of similar thickness, and depth; the exterior wall to be two feet three inches thick, and four feet below the level of the yard, in each cell there is a floor of masonry 18 inches in thickness, on which is proposed to be laid long curb-stones, ten inches thick, that extend the whole width of the cells and terminating under the partition wall, which would effectually prevent escape by excavation. The windows are inserted in the barrelled ceiling, and formed by a convex reflector of 8 inches diameter, termed *dead eyes*; this would be found to give ample light to the cells, from a position the best for ventilation and the admission of light, and a desirable one from its being out of the reach of the prisoners climbing up to escape, or to converse from one cell to that of another; the glass is hung up at the apex of a cast iron cone that is securely fixed in the solid masonry of the ceiling, and would be found a cheap and excellent window. A simple bed is provided, that is proposed to be hung against the wall to which it is made to button in the day time, with the bedding enclosed in it, out of the way. It will be understood, that the wall next the passage contains, annexed to each cell, a feeding drawer and peep-hole: the drawer is of cast-iron, six inches deep and sixteen wide, projecting a sufficient depth into the cell to form, when closed, a table of twelve inches from the surface of the wall on the inside, from which the prisoner will eat his meals. This drawer on the back, is intended to be made with a *stop*, that when drawn out by the keeper in the passage, for the purpose of depositing food or raiment, closes the aperture behind, and consequently prevents the prisoner

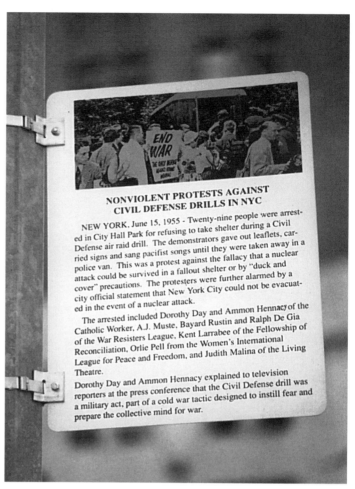

On the fourth day of the month of March in the year nineteen ninety-one, three homeless americans on this spot in lower manhattan passed a very cold and bitter night. These proud and independent people, using any material they could gather, made their own lean-to paper shelter near subterranean steam grates, drawing warmth to survive, ever watchful, that cold, cold night. By morning they were gone, leaving no trace that they had ever existed. These invisible people roamed these granite canyons forgotten and discarded by family, friends and country in the month of March in the year nineteen ninety-one.

NONVIOLENT PROTESTS AGAINST CIVIL DEFENSE DRILLS IN NYC

NEW YORK, June 15, 1955 - Twenty-nine people were arrested in City Hall Park for refusing to take shelter during a Civil Defense air raid drill. The demonstrators gave out leaflets, carried signs and sang pacifist songs until they were taken away in a police van. This was a protest against the fallacy that a nuclear attack could be survived in a fallout shelter or by "duck and cover" precautions. The protesters were further alarmed by a city official statement that New York City could not be evacuated in the event of a nuclear attack.

The arrested included Dorothy Day and Ammon Hennacy of the Catholic Worker, A.J. Muste, Bayard Rustin and Ralph De Gia of the War Resisters League, Kent Larrabee of the Fellowship of Reconciliation, Orlie Pell from the Women's International League for Peace and Freedom, and Judith Malina of the Living Theatre.

Dorothy Day and Ammon Hennacy explained to television reporters at the press conference that the Civil Defense drill was a military act, part of a cold war tactic designed to instill fear and prepare the collective mind for war.

RepoHistory,
*Lower Manhattan
Sign Project*, 1992
Photo by Tom Clem

understand its original meaning applies to site preservation as well. This suits contemporary art, which is, for better or worse, still usually an object discontinuous with its context. In museums, the past is usually roped off and under glass (or behind bars) literally and figuratively; period rooms are collected under one roof, a dizzying if dazzling array of times and places juxtaposed.

Sham ruins first appeared in Europe around 1500. The fashionable appeal of deteriorating antiques became more widespread in the upper class in the 18th century and trickled down to the middle class as an idealization of any old "old" in the 19th century. In America, ambivalence about old and new applied even to the landscape, which seemed bereft of (noneconomic) meaning to the newcomers, although of course it was rich with memory for those who had lived here for millennia. Tradition seemed to have

been lost: nouveau riche was not considered as prestigious as old money; patina made objects more valuable. At the same time, the collective inferiority complex about the newness of the "new world" accompanied a growing chauvinism. Celebration of the past has played into the hands of nationalist and conservative forces, to enforce assimilation, to "Americanize" immigrants, and to homogenize society.

At the same time, one of the contradictions in a culture that worships the new and promotes the disposable is that the older, more distant, and less comprehensible a building is, the better it fulfills a desire for something to counter or balance the new. An empty or uncomprehended symbol is more easily filled with our own meanings and fantasies. Thus historical preservation is a mirror of the present, of who we are rather than who we were; a generalized nostalgia lurks behind every quaint old house. But history itself is highly selective; it is what someone (or more likely some powerful group) has chosen to remember—usually not the mean, greedy, unjust, unfair, disastrous aspects of our collective past. Dominant cultures erase the pasts of dominated cultures. Past places and events can be used to support what is happening in the present, or they can be separated from the present in an idealized no-place, or utopia. Islands of calm, relics of a supposedly pleasanter past, such as a green, fenced square ringed by brick town-houses, dot urban seas. Time provides new contexts. The harsh realism implicit in a prison site goes against the grain.

Before they can become monuments, historic buildings are usually decontextualized, divorced from place, isolated as objects, stripped of their original reasons for being and even of their most immediate environments. Handsome old structures are devalued by being too close to a mall, a development, a rundown neighborhood, an industry, or the road itself. (A proper Bostonian of the l9th century mourned his city's failure to "trade on its great and glorious past" because its oldest buildings were now "hidden away" in unappetizing "ethnic" quarters.[5]) Historic sites may be left to fend for themselves in an incompatible and unfriendly context, like a church stranded among office buildings or the occasional little clapboard dwelling trapped in a canyon of skyscrapers. Or structures may be physically moved to a bland, neutral, or contrived new site, which is like tearing the picture in half. Even if the scape has been changed irrevocably, the land is still there. The best solution may be to emphasize the inevitable decontextualization, to wall an anachronistic place away from the rest of the world and design some sort of border passage from this world to that. The visitor could be romantically (or horribly) transported, as in a novel or film.

To become "living museums" or to be animated by art, historic sites should be collaborations with the people who made the history and/or live in the place. Martha Norkunas points out that when history is inscribed by the upper classes, everyone else participates in their own stereotyping, voluntarily (those dressed in period costumes who inhabit replicated landscapes) or involuntarily (those who go about their daily business framed by some exterior notion of "quaintness" or "authenticity"), unless they actively rebel against the process.[6]

Historical preservation and commemoration can, in fact, be hotly contested. "With so many pasts and futures making claims on us," writes Alexander Wilson, "it's hard to know which way to turn."[7] The triumphant viewpoint will represent a place, perhaps one-sidedly, for "posterity" (or for a while anyway). When there is no one to speak from first-hand experience, distortion is inevitable. Preservation is usually related to property rather than to any expansive sense of place. The Historic Sites Act of 1935 gave the green light to preservation of places where important people lived, or of architecture deemed formally important. Virtually every locale in the United States that attracts visitors is the site of a submerged struggle between the patrician elites whose history is more likely to remain visible and readable, and those who look at the undersides of the accepted texts. The furniture and bric-a-brac in these buildings often overshadow anything that can really be called history; people become historical figures by virtue of skillful acquisition. Docents and guides' spiels are clues to how a place is being officially represented, usually without the input or consent of those who live in the place. When it comes to memorializing the working classes, and especially those who rebelled against their lot, the museum establishment often seems baffled, despite the strides made by the National Industrial Park in Lowell, Massachusetts. The rise of industrial archaeology brought with it an interest in old machines, but technology rather than people's history is the crowd pleaser, with polished gears more attractive than glimpses of hard lives. Community and artist-run organizations have done better, such as New York's Chinatown History Project, Lower East Side Tenement Museum, and RepoHistory Project, the "Power of Place" project in Los Angeles, some urban "heritage trails," and the rare conscious historical society.[8]

Although such projects are generally not considered "public art," they are more effective than most work categorized as such. Public art is not the same thing as art in public places. (And debates rage about what, after all, constitutes public and private space.) Public art does not exist so that artists can plunk down work that has outgrown its native gallery habitat or indulge in their own fantasies about a place they have just parachuted into. That's private art. Nothing wrong with it, but the distinction should be made clear. Although social and local history have only recently become an issue in the mainstream arts, artists have occasionally been given the chance to resurrect aspects of the landscape and the built environment that have become invisible.

Some have focused on the on-site animation of memory and history. Among the best: Judy Baca's mural in Guadalupe, California, that traces the multicultural history of its farmworkers; Hachivi Edgar Heap of Birds' public signage about the Native American origins of urban property; Jane Greengold's "A Drop in the Bucket," a fictional/sculptural commemoration of the long disappeared Collect Pond in downtown Manhattan; Houston Conwill's shrines to the Underground Railway in towns around Buffalo, New York; Andrew Leicester's architectural mining memorials in Maryland and South Dakota; Fred Wilson's re-installations of museum collections that bring out the missing history of African Americans; RepoHistory's collective sign project in lower Manhattan which mark events that officialdom has not seen fit to commemorate; Sheila Levrant de Bretteville's biographical/memorial wall in Los Angeles to commemorate former slave Biddy Mason; Alan Sonfist's resurrection of a pre-colonial landscape in downtown New York; and the work of any number of community muralists.

These artists' approaches usually diverge drastically from that of conventional historical preservation (avoiding what Dean MacCannell calls "staged authenticity"[9]). But the goals of exhibitions like Mary Jane Jacobs' "Places With a Past" in Charleston, South Carolina in 1991 are not so dissimilar. That particular enterprise has become a model of the degrees of esthetic success and historical/connective failure inevitable when visitors try to illuminate places for the people who live there.[10] The mixed reviews by inmates and outsiders of Andrew Leicester's ambitious "Paradise" (1986) in a Cañon City, Colorado, state prison provide another cautionary tale. The artist was denied access to the inmates and therefore to any kind of collaborative input, which led to the eventual dismantling of his handsome sculpture, fountain, and garden project.[11]

There are differences between art in a prison, art for a prison, and art by prisoners. Since the 1960s, a large number of artists around the country have entered prisons as art teachers, receiving an education in exchange for one. The *"Prison Sentences"* exhibition includes some of them: Homer Jackson, Mogauwane Mahloele, John Abner, Grennan and Sperandio, and Bruce Pollock, while Jon Borofsky, Willie Cole, and James Casebere have visited and observed prison life for specific projects; others have probably at least visited people in prisons. If passing in and out of a federal penitentiary for a few hours or spending a single night in jail is as dehumanizing and as chilling to the human soul as I have found it to be, one can only imagine the horrors of long term incarceration.

Because of the implied narratives prisons contain, given all the horror movies, murder mysteries, courtroom dramas, and law-and-order TV shows we consume, they are obvious tourist attractions, both titillating and morally instructive. (Alcatraz attracts a huge number of tourists annually, in part because of the audio tour that speaks from the past in the voices of former inmates and guards.) Art's role is to complicate the story and at the same time compete with the over-simplified popular images offered in the mass media, while not losing sight of the reasons so many people want to hear the story. Artists can raise historical specters, reinstate and criticize reality, and educate through visual seduction a public that would not sit still for a history lesson.

Eastern State Penitentiary was once better known by its nickname—Cherry Hill, an appealing misnomer derived from the orchard it was built in. When a prison blooms with art, it is opened to a healing process, though that depends on a certain reciprocity between history and esthetics. Working with such haunted sites is a delicate balance, one that contemporary artists

Andrew Leicester
Paradise, 1986
Photo by Andrew Leicester

are not trained for. If the artist is concerned solely with her or his ideas or those imposed by art mainstreams, the space will simply become a repository, another museum.

At Eastern State, the monolithic stolidity of John Haviland's external architecture and its radial plan call up connections to minimalism and monuments (as well as to a flower in a walled garden). The early 19th century was called "the fancy dress ball of architecture" for its raids on the historical past. Eastern State Penitentiary's gothic fortress facade, its portcullis-like gateway suggesting some grim castle (or recalling an unenlightened and warlike past), functioned as a cautionary image. Psychological deterrence was built into its austere symbolism, modeled to some extent on the notorious Newgate Prison in London. "The exterior of a solitary prison," declared the building commissioners, "should exhibit as much as possible great strength and convey to the mind a cheerless blank indicative of the misery which awaits the unhappy being who enters within its walls." Although penitentiaries (as opposed to mere prisons) were optimistically planned as places for repentance, Eastern State was intended from the beginning "to produce, by means of sufferings principally acting on the mind and accompanied with moral and religious instruction, a disposition to virtuous conduct, the only sure preventive of crime." If this didn't work, the penitentiary was supposed to impress "so great a dread and terror" as to preclude further violations.

The generalized notion of imprisonment coupled with the imposing architectural spaces proffer an exciting armature for art. The specific lives and stories will be harder to exhume. Norman Johnston says that Eastern State, which received its first inmate in October 1829, "must be considered the most influential prison ever built and arguably the American building most widely imitated in Europe and Asia in the nineteenth century....Next to democratic government, Philadelphia's most important export [was] methods for penology."[12] Yet reading the recent historical catalogue *Eastern State Penitentiary: Crucible of Good Intentions* (from which I have inferred the title of this essay), I was struck by its total exclusion of human voices. Not even the wardens' experiences are quoted, and the voices of guards, visitors,

inmates, and relatives are silent. The women incarcerated in Eastern State until 1923 and the prison's interracial history (it was quietly desegregated only in the 1960s) are barely mentioned.

The recuperation of stories is an integral part of personal and family and communal histories. Prison stories are harder to come by because of social stigma, but they are also prompted by sensationalism. Prison diaries or letters from Cherry Hill's 142 years are probably scarce due to illiteracy, and the researcher must depend on the plethora of print devoted to prison reform over the last century. The rarer body of first-person material is available only to those able to access the hundreds of hours of audio and video interviews, which are publicly available in Philadelphia.

This is saddening because today is a particularly auspicious moment for looking at the history of prisons in this country. Eastern State Penitentiary's own history of attempted reforms contrasts painfully with current statistics. Over one and a half million people are in U.S. prisons, one of the largest populations in the world; and it is growing daily. Economic and racial gaps continue to widen. The proliferation of "control-unit" prisons marks the return of general solitary confinement as practiced in Cherry Hill's early years. (Florence, Colorado, is the most recent addition to their ranks.) The barbaric death penalty has been revived in several states. As I write, Pennsylvania is the storm center around one of the most important, and most disputed, death-row cases of the decade, that of journalist Mumia Abu-Jamal.

While the hatches of human warehouses are battened down for a long siege, correctional policies are fueled by fear and vengeance. Any impulse toward reform appears to have given way to pure social control. Art that manages to climb the walls has its work cut out for it in such a national context. It can hardly compete physically with its surroundings. But it can reflect on the social meaning of constriction, freedom, violence, and claustrophobia. The "sense of place," a popular art subject these days, usually connotes more harmonious circumstances, but displacement is a component of place, and prisons offer unique views of alienation and the nature of solitude. (Prison has been described as "a monastery inhabited by men who do not choose to be monks.") The lives of the six staff families that lived within the walls, including the warden, must reveal rich subtexts to publicly stated goals. And consider the roles of religion (forced down the craws of early prisoners), education and literacy (the eventual establishment at Eastern of a library of over 10,000 volumes), labor history, as reflected in conflicts between unions and cheap prison labor, and the mental and physical illnesses produced by correctional institutions.

In the end, the Eastern State Penitentiary was considered a failure. (What prison is not?) By the Depression, according to Jeffrey A. Cohen, it "was no longer a monument to the promise of rehabilitation. It had become a fatalistic part of the correctional bureaucracy, a warehouse for the state's toughest convicts. Little of the founders' optimism about human nature or the philanthropic tenor of its original governance survived."[13] At the same time, Cherry Hill has worked its way up the landmark hierarchy. Designated as a historic site by the city of Philadelphia in 1958, it became a National Historic Landmark in 1965 and was placed on the State Register of Historic Places in 1970. When the last prisoners were taken away early in 1971, the future seemed to hold demolition or development. Unlike a former New York City Police Headquarters, the building will not be turned inside out, into condos and boutiques. Instead, it will survive, thanks to local communities and academics and because it would have been too much trouble to tear down or remodel.

Although functionally obsolete, Cherry Hill constitutes an architectural memoir of good intentions, a collective social symbol to be compared with contemporary morality. The sunny Disneyfication and homogenization that prevails at so many historical sites will fortunately be hard to pull off at Eastern State. It is a site of pain and a reflection of social turmoil, justice and injustice. Its emotive aura can only be watered down by historification, but it is not too late to bring to the foreground all those hitherto inaudible voices. Artists can connect the potent relics of places from the past with the people and places that we see around us today. While many of us enjoy looking at "old things" for their own sake, many more of us would like to have access to resources that help us understand our own complicity with history, where we fit into a cohesive picture. Maps and archives and historical sites can be reinvented. Artists can lead the way.

Lucy R. Lippard is a writer and activist based in New Mexico and Maine who has published seventeen books on contemporary art and one novel. Her most recent books are The Pink Glass Swan: Selected Essays on Feminist Art *(1995),* Partial Recall: Photographs of Native North Americans *(1992, and* Mixed Blessings: New Art in a Multicultural America *(1990).*

Photo by Todd Gilens

1 This text was adapted from a section on historical preservation from my forthcoming book *The Lure of the Local* (New York: The New Press, 1996).

2 Raymond Williams, quoted in Christina Kreps, *Museums and Promoting Cross-Cultural Awareness,* paper presented at 1987 ICME conference in Leiden, Holland, p.1.

3 Kevin Lynch, *What Time is This Place?*, Cambridge, Mass.: MIT Press, 1972.

4 J.B. Jackson, *The Necessity for Ruins*, Amherst: University of Massachusetts Press, 1980, p.101.

5 Stuart Mais, quoted in John A. Jakle, *The Tourist: Travel in Twentieth Century North America,* Lincoln: University of Nebraska Press, 1985, p.287.

6 Martha K. Norkunas, *The Politics of Public Memory*, Albany: State University of New York Press, 1993.

7 Alexander Wilson, *The Culture of Nature*, Cambridge, Mass.: Blackwell, 1992, p.208.

8 See Dolores Hayden, *The Power of Place: Urban Landscapes as Public History,* Cambridge, Mass.: MIT Press, 1995, for a particularly intelligent overview of many such sites.

9 See Dean MacCannell, the dean indeed of writing on tourism and historical "authenticity," *The Tourist,* New York, Schocken Books, 1976 and Empty Meeting Grounds, London/New York: Routledge, 1992.

10 A lavish book about the exhibition was published by Rizzoli (New York) in 1991.

11 See Erika Doss, *Spirit Poles and Flying Pigs,* Washington, D.C.: Smithsonian Institution Press, 1995, p. 23-24, and Lucy R. Lippard in *Z Magazine,* May, 1989.

12 All quotations and historical facts about Cherry Hill not otherwise referenced are from Norman Johnston with Kenneth Finkel and Jeffrey A. Cohen, *Eastern State Penitentiary: Crucible of Good Intentions,* Philadelphia: Philadelphia Museum of Art for the Eastern Penitentiary Task Force of the Preservation Coalition of Greater Philadelphia, 1994.

13 *Ibid.*, p. 181-82.

"Site-Specific Prison Vision"

Eileen Neff

The first effect is stunning, an unexpected door on light and time the building's dense facade does not admit. Skylights penetrate the vaulted ceilings of each corridor and evoke a hallowed space, an architecture that would redeem. With its prison functions ended in 1971, Eastern State Penitentiary is well on its entropic journey back to nature and very far from the ideal vision of its original planners. But, then again, it always had been. This exultant space was, at the start, lost on the prisoners, who were required to wear hoods over their heads whenever they left the isolation of their single cells. Yet, the cells, too, were and remain strangely beautiful and monastic on a smaller scale, adding to the accumulation of paradoxical responses that today's visit to ESP inspires. Forgetting for a moment that the prisoner's isolation was imposed, one can imagine such a simple, private space, each with its own sky-lit dome, as a place one might choose, to be alone and to learn from. If one could choose. But what is known about the reality of prison life soon replaces the drifting imagination and fills these empty spaces with yet another, darker image to experience. By turns, the hard facts and strange beauty of the prison push their way to the front of one's thoughts.

The peeling walls expose their own exhaustion and the colors of another time. The abandoned cells create a series of stages for the poetics of natural decay: a metal bed frame lies on its side, alone in an empty cell; a back wall has separated itself like a tombstone lit by the daylight behind; a back wall has crumbled and opened the space, inviting the outside in. Ailanthus and paulownia trees have made their way through the weakened walls as if to reclaim what was always theirs. One wonders if the cherry trees might even return.[1] (Do we even wish that they would?) We feel, in the presence of this site, how the wild advance of nature moves us, draws its destruction and regeneration to an aesthetic height and reveals, as an artist would, some inexorable truth.

THE MANY TRUTHS OF ESP

Perhaps, with these thoughts in mind, we can best approach the fourteen art projects commissioned for ESP and understand why artists were invited to explore the complex nature of this site. Their own often marginal status in society suggests an ironic link that, while not accounting for their presence here, reinforces this site's refusal to be read in only one way.[2] Whether working out of society's darkest corners or celebrated at its cultural center, the artist remains a vital figure for our lives. The presentation of these site-generated art works is a fitting transitional acknowledgment of the reflective moment that currently surrounds ESP as its fate is being decided. No longer the prison it was and not yet whatever it will become, the site is a perfect arena of possibilities in which the artist can raise important questions and make his imagination our own.

As an inverse reaction to the visual impact of ESP, Homer Jackson and Mogauwane Mahloele (in collaboration with Lloyd Lawrence, Richard Jordan, and John Abner) were driven to create "Why Malcolm Had to Read." It's not that they didn't recognize its uncanny beauty, but among them they had spent many years working in prisons, and the hard facts of their experience made the aesthetic distance that the building

strips that hang like a ritual curtain on this theater of prison life. As described in the project's proposal notes, "a 15- to 20-minute, continuous loop, audio collage, consisting of sound effects, ambient sound, dialogue, music, poetry/prose, letters, interviews, monologues, theatrical reenactments in English, Spanish, Xhosa, Sotho, and Zulu . . ."[3] is a real and fictive mix that strengthens the silence of the installation's inspiring image, the transformative experience of Malcolm X imprisoned. It raises the question of how one could survive let alone transcend this maddening, endless clamor. It also recalls, by its difference, the description of sound control in ESP's earliest days:

Violation of the rules prohibiting communication or unnecessary noise, such as singing or whistling, could result in the denial of dinner, the main meal of the day, for a week. Guards wore socks over their shoes and the wheels of the carts that brought food to the cells were covered with leather to ensure silence in which the prisoners' attempts to communicate could be overheard. Visitors sometimes commented on the unearthly silence inside the prison.[4]

inspires an impossible position to sustain. Jackson talks about his discomfort in watching the ease with which visitors walk through the empty prison. Just as people have lied about prison life, so too, he feels, the building lies and provokes these artists to speak about other realities.

Their collaboration engages an entire cell block with a pulsating concert of sound and sights whose feverish pitch is like a high school at recess or a functioning prison. The disembodied sounds of this installation reach its visitors before they pass through the black X painted on clear plastic

As for many of the artists working in *Prison Sentences,* the natural theatrics of the prison site were too inviting for Jackson and Mahloele not to engage. Focusing on the incarceration of men and women of color throughout the world, their project reinvents an idea of prison life, using ESP as a universal stage that reaches beyond its own particular history. Paralleling the combined use of actual and invented elements in the sound tracks, the visual elements bring their own amalgam of fact and imagination. The inherent repetition of life in prison becomes a primary metaphor in this collaboration. Black plaques punctuate the cell block walls in commemorative procession, each one inscribed with a specific inmate's story, naming names and dates, their fictitious origin not revealed to the viewer. Anonymous faces or eyes appear on black painted cell doors, another repeated element reinforcing the inevitable drama of cell after cell, day after day—the literal figure of repetition that bears so much symbolic weight. Inside the individual cells, a wide range of narratives explore the rage and horror as well as the great humanity of life imprisoned. Here, too, repetition is often used. One cell retains its metal bed which is covered with a layer of white bread slices. On a nearby stool, a pyramid of water jars is piled, the daily rations of sustenance and time; groups of counting marks cover the wall. In another cell, eight shaving mirrors hang from the walls at eye level. The floor is tiled like a pool of water in mirrored squares, reflecting the whole sad cell. Other cells are more literally descriptive, offering their still tableaux as a museum would. Recalling images from the artists' experiences, one cell evokes a torture chamber, another displays a hangman's noose.

Homer Jackson, et al.
Why Malcolm Had to Read

Together, these images create a powerful yet contradictory effect, feeding the visitor's fascination and curiosity while moving him along—as if to escape the feel of prison life breathing down his neck.

Expressing another idea of theater, Christina Kubisch's project comes literally and figuratively from the other side of the world. This Berlin artist's light and sound installations conflate natural and technological processes to evoke the multiple rewards of sheer presence. The striking differences between the richly layered collaborative spirit of "Why Malcolm Had to Read" and the singular vision of "Skylights" draw a likely yet in some ways unexpected parallel. In both works, the sound is experienced first. Whereas the collaboration filled the space with layers of talk and noise and music, Kubisch's minimal, dark composition played on a glass armonica invites the listener to fill in the empty, evocative space that it leaves. Visually, it's much the same: of the twenty-four cells that Kubisch engages, all have been emptied of left-over furniture, and twelve on one side of the cellblock have been left as the artist found them. On the other side, the cells have been altered only by the addition of an ultraviolet light that hangs from the ceiling of each cell in which the skylight has been covered. In the description of her project, the artist points to the original uses of ultraviolet light, which include criminal investigations, restoration of paintings, and interplanetary space exploration, uses that examine the always present but invisible layers that surround us.

Throughout the prison, the natural decay of the building offers, without artistic intervention, an invitation to further scrutiny.

Christina Kubisch
Skylights

In these darkened, empty, artificially lit rooms, Kubisch means to reveal the metaphorical possibilities of this physical phenomenon by simple acts of light and sound to heighten our perception. In this apparently vacant environment, seeing becomes the deeper, more mysterious experience that we associate with the night and our own invisible selves. It is the domain of memory and the imagination—of the lives spent here mingling with our passing presence—which could fill up these spaces as any extended collaboration might. Except that you can't "see" it. And unless you lose yourself in it, you wouldn't think so. Across the corridor in Kubisch's project, the day light works its own magic.

Bruce Pollock
Vas Hermeticus

"ONE DOES NOT

BECOME

ENLIGHTENED BY

IMAGINING

FIGURES OR LIGHT,

BUT BY MAKING

THE DARKNESS

CONSCIOUS"

C.G. Jung

Bruce Pollock begins his notes for "Vas Hermeticus" with a quote from Carl Jung, which speaks to the entire prison project. For Pollock, it informs the symbolic relationship he wishes to draw between the spiritual journey that ESP's designing fathers intended for its prisoners and the transformative powers of the hermetic art of alchemy. Pollock points out that Hermes is not only the god of alchemy and magic but also the god of thieves and criminals. The artist's understanding of these ideas is also reinforced by his experience working as an artist in the prison system.

"Vas Hermeticus" uses three cells. One is sealed off, the "sealed vessel" of the title, with stratified layers of its own plaster debris into which a green prison bench has been embedded, an effective analog for the body imprisoned. The profile of the bench suggests the letter "A" and is meant to

signal the beginning of the prisoners' journey. One wants to call the cell to its right "the red cell" for the astonishing richness of the earth revealed, the result of tree roots having grown through the cell walls, causing the disintegration of their plaster coating. All of the debris in the cell has been sifted and swept into a circular cone in the center. A corner of a metal bed has been caught in the circle. A small round piece of daylight moves across the floor, and, like the conical debris, draws the viewer's gaze up and out the small round skylight of the cell. On the rear wall, Pollock has carved a labyrinth which configures its symbolic presence, as the artist imagines it, beneath the penitentiary floors. In the corner of the cell, a bottle of sulfur-based medicine found in the dispensary sits on the floor. In this esoteric installation, the invisible correspondences do not always rise to the surface. As for all of

Winifred Lutz
Serving Time
(Cell thresholds marked, left to right,
Doing Time, Marking Time, and
Making Time.)
Photos by Gregory Benson

Pollock's choices, the connection here is alchemical, as sulfur is one of the three key elements of alchemy, its symbolic significance being the generative power of light and fire. Across the corridor, an inverse image—the swept debris stays close to the walls, leaving an empty oval in the center of the cell—completes this three-part installation. In Pollock's words: "I brought nothing in from outside, my material was only what was available on the site. The rest is alchemy." The alchemical language of this project may be obscure, but the simple gestures of the artist, sweeping and shaping what is before him, suggest a parallel image of the prisoner and his need for personal transformation.

The idea of the artist as conscious attendant implied in Pollock's work is made manifest by Winifred Lutz. Pollock has moved through the cells of his installation as the invisible instrument of the alchemical powers he wishes to reveal; Lutz, in a play on prison talk, serves time.

Inherent in Lutz's response to the prison is a critique of the moral authority embodied in the building's structure, the physical arrogance that assumes time can be stopped, and that prisoners' transforma-

tion can be achieved through isolation and seclusion. In Lutz's hands, the building's inevitable vulnerability to change and decay is illuminated through the most subtle and ongoing acts of Nature, which undermine the enforced control that the architecture meant to express.

Initially drawn to the fact that the prisoners used their individual exercise yards as gardens, Lutz brings the same spirit of attendance and regeneration to a notion of Time. This is variously explored in three successive cells, each with its own meaning and title engraved in a bluestone threshold at the foot of the entrance door. "Marking Time," the center cell, is the only one the visitor may enter. Lutz has replastered the walls and painted everything white. Only the iron door frame around what was the entrance to the exercise yard is left alone, a dark frame for the decision to cement the yard door closed. To emphasize the original spiritual intentions of these monkish cells, gold leaf covers the skylight fascia. In the restored condition of the cell, one can trace the slow but steady accumulation of time making its marks. Water silently seeps through the walls and foot prints subtly

Malcolm Cochran
Soliloquy

accumulate. The artist, like the prisoner, participates in the rituals of time. Returning once each week, Lutz repeatedly paints the word INTIME on the inside wall that frames the door—the wall the warden would not see—in a reddish paint made of cell siftings. The words grow from the floor toward the ceiling like rows of bricks, casting a deeper pink glow into the cell as they accumulate.

The viewer is kept out of the two side cells by a fine mesh screening. In the cell to the right, Lutz has covered the floor and metal bed frame with a light coating of flour, which reveals the decay of the scraped walls and the slow advance of the blue-green mold on the floor. Only the back wall is plastered and engraved with a drawing of a modified prison plan that has a life of its own: Lutz regularly treats its incised lines with a mixture of flour, water, and mold that she collects from the bed and floor. The mold will grow and obliterate the image of the prison, an analog for the decay of the prison itself. In the left-hand cell, Lutz has created her own garden, the image of her original inspiration. Moss covers the floor, and the collected cell debris serves to hold a small ailanthus tree, known as the Tree of Heaven, yet

because of its rapid growth, also called the tree from hell. It grows toward the skylight and, in time, it will block the skylight out.

NARRATIVE TIME

Another image of time passing mingles with the physical evidence of the artist's labor, symbolically configured as a 75 foot vine-like braid of hair in "Soliloquy." Malcolm Cochran creates visual narratives that raise ordinary objects to metaphoric heights by the intensity of his poetic concentration. In this work, Chinese horse tails are used to suggest a braid of human hair which acknowledges Cochran's earliest impressions of ESP when he, like Lutz, was struck by the wild growth of ailanthus trees pushing their way through the abandoned cells. It was also during his first tour of the prison that he learned of the women who had served time there.

The braided hair begins like a sleeping head lying on the metal prison bed and works its way up and out of the skylight, across the roof of the cell and over the prison yard to the outside prison wall. In the telling, the braid draws a predictable line of escape. Experienced, the segmented sequence only comes together as the

Willie Cole
5 to 10

Telling a different story, Willie Cole infuses the invisible with a level of reality to create a fiction that speaks about the real world. It's a shadowy story of unseen children and lost lives whose traces he evokes in a collection of used and discarded playground equipment within the prison yard. With their broken, spent demeanor, these objects sit comfortably in this site, as if they had fallen into disrepair along with the prison building. It takes only a few symbolic gestures for Cole to push these complacent images beyond our recognition and into the poetics of the impossible. One set of swings is trapped against the perimeter wall; in another, the chains appear shackled together. The slide is upside-down and the sandbox is filled with the turned up soles (souls?) of children's sneakers, as if they were buried there. In each situation, the metaphorical images that point both in and out of the prison walls are held together by a culture of violence. Across from Death Row, Cole has hung six basketball hoops along the top of the 30 foot yard wall, another ironic image that identifies the sport as a cultural escape and, at the same time, places it clearly out of reach.

With their proximity to Death Row, Cole also sees the hoops as halos, the prisoners' spirits rising in the air. Less ethereal are the sneakers thrown over the window frames of Death Row, and others bunched together like some awful knot hanging from a playground fragment. With "5 to 10," Cole extends the abandoned stage of the prison to speak about the abandoned lives that lead there. The visitor walks among these sad signs with a feeling of resignation not unlike that of the children and, ultimately, the prisoners that these two-way signs point to.

memory of each part is recalled. For Cochran, the memory of its trail includes the book of his daughter's from which he learned how to braid. It also recalls his grandmother who lived with him when he was a child, who braided rugs as well as her own hair. In the cell, the fixed image only suggests the braid's full length, discovered later in the prison yard. Most pressing is the palpable presence of a disembodied figure, a woman, asleep and lost in prison time. Expanding the significance of this image, a small video of a woman braiding and unbraiding her hair appears as a mirrored reflection in the adjacent cell. Todd Gilens, in the exhibition brochure, notes that "the prisoners' separation also meant that common experiences like the parallel images this work presents, could never be shared, or even known." In this sense, Cochran's work stretches beyond his specific fiction to the myriad stories told by the artists at ESP.

THE SHIFTING ROLE OF THE VIEWER

As if to break the impossible circle drawn by Willie Cole, Fiona Templeton has created "Cells of Release," an interactive installation that uses the natural symbolism of the prison to stage her collaboration with Amnesty International. There is very little artifice here. Each cell has a modest arrangement of the original cell furniture along with some written and photographic information on current prisoners of conscience. Included with this material are petitions through which the public can act on the prisoners' behalf. Symbolically linking the isolated cells and representing the only apparent sign of the artist, a long white paper ribbon carrying a line of text weaves its way through the cells and throughout the cell block. Written on the site over a period of six weeks, cell by cell and day by day, this poetic meditation on isolation patterns itself after the monotony of prison time. Despite the linear progression of the text, the viewer is free to read or not read at any point throughout the installation; likewise, regarding the implicit invitation to interact by signing Amnesty petitions. It is the viewer's freedom, exaggerated in the context of the prison and reinforced by the parade of incarcerated faces pictured in the cells, that quickens his sense of responsibility in what would ordinarily be a passive role.

A heightened awareness of the viewer's or spectator's identity is a familiar theme for Templeton, who fashioned one of her most compelling performance pieces, "You—The City," around the concept of a single spectator being guided through a journey of people and places within a city. In the same spirit of nontraditional contemporary performance, "Cells of Release" proceeds without familiar theatrical trappings and subtly implicates its audience.

Although contemporary performance work is as varied as the artists working in the field, it has, in many of its expressions, reconfigured the traditional relationships between actors or stage and the audience. In the Happenings of the late 1950s and 1960s, theatrical expectations were turned upside-down, engaging the viewer through frustration and discomfort. Earlier, related precedents can be found in Futurist and Dada productions, which confronted the viewer with verbal abuse. Templeton's tone, established by the strong political content and apparent lack of theatrics, belies this aggressive history but participates in it nonetheless. The viewer is no longer just watching, but may be called on at any moment to perform.

Beth B illuminates that moment for the visitor at ESP as soon as her installation is entered. "A Holy Experiment" has the audience re-enact two of the underlying principles of prison life—confinement and surveillance. Visitors who walk into this two-cell installation become unwitting participants, finding themselves suddenly locked behind an electronically operated door or watching from the adjacent cell as other visitors' temporary confinement is broadcast on a video monitor. The experience in the locked cell has its natural discomfort and requires trust in the reality of the art context for one's imminent release. In the open cell, where one is in apparent control, it is difficult not to question who else may be watching now. "A Holy Experiment," written in neon around the constructed facade of the mechanical door, quotes the language that was used in the early days of ESP and attracts the viewer like a movie marquee. Beside each door sits a metal table with candles and incense and a printed handout that comments on the insanity of confinement and surveillance. Complimenting this text is a sound track of several voices that implore, threaten, preach, and question the same issues. All of these dramatic effects support the central theme of the project, whose primary impact is delivered through the phenomenological encounter experienced by the visitor turned player on this natural prison stage.

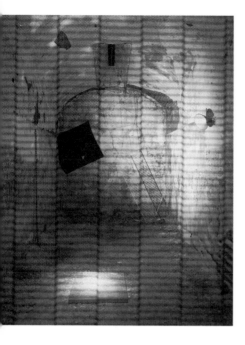  

ANOTHER KIND OF THEATER

Carolyn Healy and
John Phillips
Overtones

Just as the disembodied recordings of prisoners' voices first greeted the visitor in the Jackson/Mahloele collaboration as an invitation and accompaniment to their narrative installation, so does an eerie computerized montage of natural and synthetic sounds pull the visitor into the darkened cellblock of "Overtones," where a corresponding series of abstract tableaux awaits. It is worth pausing over the moment of approach to Carolyn Healy's and John Phillips' installation, to watch those before you almost disappear into the relative darkness, wondering if someone will be watching you—shades of "A Holy Experiment," perhaps. Inside, the central experience of this 27 cell project places the viewer in a more traditional relationship to a museum practice of individual period rooms or dioramas that may not be entered but only looked at and, in this case, listened to.

Each cell serves as a dramatic frame for the studied arrangements of form and light that were conceived in a full-scale cell model in Healy's studio. Included are some identifiable objects like crab traps and a folding baby crib, although most of the forms are fragments of possible objects, like poles and rods, cone shapes and brass bars, metal spirals and sheets of glass.

Paralleling Healy's sculptural decisions, Phillips devised a series of water- and dust-proof analog chips to carry the sound effects he developed. Together, their visual and auditory response to this site reflects an internalization of the psychology of prison life and recalls an Abstract Expressionist practice in which the image and its meaning arise from an intensely personal space. A metaphorical relationship is assumed between the shapes and colors, the angles and edges of objects and a wide range of human emotions. In the Modernist tradition, the art image is proclaimed for its power to heal. Isolation, confinement, fear, sorrow, and even hope are explored through these formal compositions of sight and sound. Some of the simplest, illuminating the cell itself, are the most compelling: a large wad of black netting nearly fills one cell; an indecipherable white form mysteriously hangs behind the screen-covered entrance of another. The theatrical lighting that visually enhances each arrangement takes an isolated stand in one cell where a circle of light sits on the empty floor. Behind a line of metal chain linking the cells and separating the viewers, the artists, through an empathetic transcription of emotion, make their presence known.

Jonathon Borofsky
Dark Flying Figure for
Eastern State Penitentiary
Photo by Todd Gilens
On Opposite page:
Dream Room

PICTURING THE ARTIST

The extensive variety of responses to ESP point not only to the resonant content of this historical and physical site but also to the contemporary plurality of artists' sensibilities and practices. Prominent among them is the esthetic scrutiny of the "context" of art, the language of presentation framed by the gallery and museum, and reframed by non-traditional art sites such as this prison. This self-reflexive view may also include an investigation of the artist as depicted within these defining frames. Even in such a historically saturated environment as ESP, several different pictures of the artist have been drawn.

The personal identification and transformation experienced and expressed by Healy and Phillips begins to speak of the private self in ways that other artists in this project condense into more explicit, psychologically narrative images, images

one might encounter in a dream. Since the 1970s, Jonathan Borofsky has been publicly celebrating his dreams as a fecund pool of inspirational images where his private psyche meets and mingles with the great archetypes of a universal imagination. One of these images, "Dark Flying Figure," hangs high behind the front gate of the prison, a black looming presence whose outstretched arms cannot reach beyond their fixed position. The prison context reinforces the idea of escape or release, but a more passive posture of hovering and watching is also suggested. Inside one of the prison cells, Borofsky has drawn and written out two of his dream images on opposing front and back walls. The rough execution of the off-handed style supports the viewer's inclination to see these images and words as the work of a former prisoner who felt compelled to record his dreams. One reads,

43

Simon Grennan and
Christopher Sperandio
Life In Prison

"I dreamed blacks were marching for freedom and one girl said she would tell the truth." The other begins, "Falling back to sleep again, I envisioned the top part of my head removed," and includes a drawing of the top part of his head, a characteristically autobiographical image. Borofsky's self-reflective practice took a documentary form in 1985 when he made "Prisoners," a video of very personal interviews with thirty-two imprisoned men and women. It's a very sympathetic series of portraits exposing

childhood traumas and broken dreams as well as dreams still held by the prisoners. It points, like all of Borofsky's work, to the complex question of what it means to be free, a question which, in the context of the prison, might fill our waking hours as well as our dreams.

Simon Grennan and Christopher Sperandio include themselves and the origins of their prison project within the first few pages of "Life in Prison," a comic book of prison stories they created for *Prison Sentences*. These collaborators have always been interested in engaging nontraditional art audiences within the local communities where they have produced their work. Here they depict themselves as regular guys: Chris Sperandio is on tour at ESP with Julie Courtney and Todd Gilens, the exhibition curators (also drawn into the picture), and realizes this might be an opportunity to produce the comic book he and Grennan had thought about before; Chris Sperandio is back in New York, pulling his pants up with one hand, the other on the phone to Simon Grennan, his London-based collaborator, the two of them working out the details of how they'll proceed. The question of gathering material is quickly answered through Sperandio's brother's prison experience and their former connections at Strangeways, a prison in Manchester, England, modeled after ESP, where in 1993 they began a photography project with a group of inmates. The stories touch on some classic themes: the lure and reality of gangsterhood as portrayed in films and lived

in real prison life; the stupid mistake that gets one thirty days and a new resolve to never repeat the prison experience; the humanity of the criminals turned songwriters and singers who, for a moment, become prison stars. These few small stories, within the frame of the reduced and yet exaggerated comic book format (which includes the requisite "bam" and "kerunch"), become emblematic of the countless prison stories there are to be told. On sale at the exhibition's entrance, the book becomes an art object that the audience of this exhibition can take home. It also provides a context for these co-creators to announce their own sensibility and the nature of their practice as part of the content of their creation.

Virgil Marti responds to the prison site through an identification with another artist's story. He uses the trial and imprisonment of Oscar Wilde to consider the relationship of nature and culture as it generally relates to the basic premise of reform at ESP

(solitary confinement will make you good) and as it specifically comments on questions of homosexuality (what Marti refers to as nature vs. nurture). Commemorating the 100th year anniversary of Wilde's imprisonment for "acts of gross indecency," the centennial of his forced "outing," this esthetically driven project treats the subject as Marti imagines Wilde would have. Outside the door of the cell block, a patch of sunflowers stands guard; a ceramic sunflower plaque quotes the libelous calling card that instigated the trial:

For Oscar Wilde, posing sodomite
Marquis of Queensberry

Inside, a carefully arranged spread of silk lilies, in a textured conversation with the peeling walls, cover the cellblock floor and leave a winding path to Wilde's commemorative cell. The shift from the natural to the artificial is pure Wilde, considering both, and choosing the latter. The loss of individuality that each prisoner

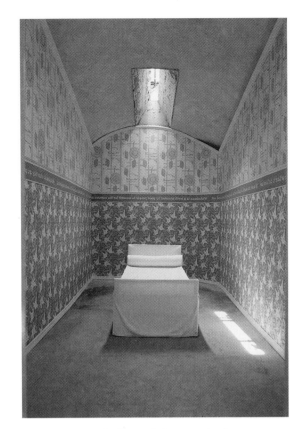

Virgil Marti
For Oscar Wilde

must suffer is dramatized here as Marti symbolically reinvents a cell for Wilde. Acknowledging Wilde's love of the surface and the superficial—"it is only the superficial qualities that last"—Marti covered the walls with sheetrock and hand-printed wall paper, inspired by Arts and Crafts designs, a sunflower pattern printed above and a lily pattern below. In between, in keeping with the prison's concept of forced contemplation, quotes from Wilde's writings surround the viewer at eye level. Where the papered wall meets the unfinished ceiling, a strip of white molding skirts the top edge like a hoop with which one might lift this temporary, artificial cell skin. In the center of the cell, Marti has slipped a fitted white velveteen cover over a metal prison bed. The horizontal slats of the frame read like ribs pressing against the thin cover, a ghostly portrait of the incarcerated artist stripped bare.

In his proposal for this project, Marti notes that within three weeks of Wilde's two-year incarceration, the press reported that he had gone mad. Presenting this special case of the artist imprisoned

serves to remind us of that particular Victorian moment while causing us to reflect on this contemporary moment of our own.

Each project, in its own way, has made the prisoner's experience the focus of its inquiry, implying if not directly stating an empathy for the imagined difficulties of the prisoners' lives. The first sign that James Casebere has shifted this focus comes with his selecting an installation site that was not a prison cell but an irregularly shaped room near the prison's center that might have served some administrative purpose. As if in preparation for the point of view he assumes in this installation, Casebere has been overseeing the production and documentation of public buildings as controlled environments, most recently including a series of prisons, and most pointedly including this prison, through model scale constructions that he builds only in order to photograph. The models are austerely poetic, sacrificing architectural detailing for the psychological impact of the reduced forms exposed in their highly staged light. More than one critic has noted how the obsession of this labor-intensive

James Casebere
The Model Room

project implicates the artist, as model maker, as part of the apparent subject. It is this "fictional" artist, the prison designer, that Casebere addresses in "The Model Room." A wooden table structure attached to the angled walls holds the remains of plaster models, half buried in the room's natural decay, half strewn about as if by their mad maker. A plaster legend of nine different prison plans hangs on the wall. In Casebere's original proposal for this room, a more detailed portrayal of the artist/planner and his obsessive desire to control the prisoners was outlined. It included hanging photographs of wanted men, collections of criminal pictures and books about the criminal mind to "represent the enemy in pictures." Casebere's decision to leave this psychological embellishment out of the final image reminds us of the choices he must make to create the stark, featureless impressions of his photographed models. The viewer wanders into this spare site of the artist's mind and can only imagine.

The concept of control that Casebere's prison-designing artist is driven by, and ultimately suffers the loss of, is advanced by Allan Wexler as the individual's true salvation. How the individual surrounds himself, shapes and is shaped by the objects—the housing, the furniture, the

"things"—with which he occupies the world, is at the center of Wexler's poetic inquiry. His work suggests that as the imagination informs these relationships, so might the individual exercise a kind of control. The individual that Wexler proposes for this task at ESP is the artist himself. The isolated cell is the challenge the artist can rise to. The wistful possibility, considered at this essay's beginning, of seeing the invitation of these cells as a place one might choose to be alone and to learn from, is taken up by Wexler in his version of "Cell." Minus the "smell of the freshly planed pine door jambs" (and lots of other, obvious particulars) that Wexler values in Thoreau's retreat to Walden Pond, "Cell" becomes this artist's opportunity to explore the examined and examining life of self-imposed solitude. An initial leap of imagination (and freedom) allows Wexler to fashion a cell within the cell, an insulated, dropped ceiling, a cleaned up interior featuring its own heater, portable toilet, new sink and small air conditioner. It's as if he decided to secure some basic comforts before getting down to the business of how this now even smaller than original cell might be lived in by his fictive artist. Unable to build a full-scale model in his too-short studio, Wexler worked within the outlined dimensions taped to his studio floor. His first thoughts were to keep this simulated cell/studio experience as autobiographical and limited as possible. Out of his daily routine of brown bagged lunches and deliveries of breakfast and dinner by the local diner, Wexler developed a unique palette of forms and materials from which the imagined practice of the isolated artist would grow. He allowed himself a few necessary objects including a pencil, broom, toothbrush and paste, toilet paper and soap. The brown lunch bags became writing surfaces for the list of tools to be made. First he would make the tools and then he would make the art. The broom became a critical source of wood and straw and even a nail, which he removed from the broom handle using the zipper handle from his pants. Adding the delivered soda can metal and his toothbrush handle, Wexler developed an astonishing assortment of tools—a selection of knives, a rasp, hammer, pen, saw and, of course, many small brushes. Aluminum take-out dishes were reconfigured into paper makers, and water-soaked toilet paper, reduced to pulp, became the source for new drawing paper. Or sheets of toilet paper were laminated together with evaporated milk glue to create a drawing surface or slippers that would sit at the foot of the prison bed. Coffee, sugar and milk created a watercolor set; ketchup, mustard and jelly provided the primary colors. The soap was transformed into crayons or carved into small shapes for building. The list goes on. All of these handmade objects were installed in the reconstructed cell: the color charts were hung on the wall; the tools and fabricated cups and utensils were placed around the cell like small sculptures. The toothbrush and toothpaste sit neatly aligned on their shelf.

Allan Wexler
Cell

Hanging on the wall behind them, fourteen drawings of other possible arrangements remind us of how obsessive such concentrated attention can be.

As a final gesture, Wexler sealed off the cell with a Plexiglas wall, confirming the artifice of his image, now perceived as a period room in a museum—a museum celebrating the imagination of the artist. The viewer's physical distance reinforces the symbolic posture of the work as it embraces isolation and limitation and frames the transformation of ordinary objects and actions of every day.

"Cell" also reaches beyond its own intentions and becomes an ironic paradigm for the artworks at ESP. It locates and fixes an idea of the artist whose traditional practice is informed by the possibility of being sanctioned in the "museum," as "Cell" wittily suggests it has. It also identifies the prison and museum as the parallel public institutions of authority and control that they are. Further, it points to the present status of Eastern State Penitentiary, which is best characterized by the simultaneous decline and development of its physical and historical presence—its actual cultural context. Other artists here have referenced the language of museum exhibitions with contradictory effect. Although Jackson and

Mahloele use the natural frames of the cells to isolate and orient their various tableaux, the prison context defies the artificial displacement associated with museum display. Even in Healy's and Phillips' museum-informed, highly abstracted presentations, it is the symbolic content of the prison that inspires the work. The power structure implicit in the museum is explicitly revealed in the prison as it exerts its leftover influence on each artist. While the building continues to deteriorate, the artworks incorporate the temporal flux of the site, confirming the significance of site-specific productions and contributing another layer to the textured history of the prison. The artist, even in this paradoxical, nontraditional art setting, remains the one who persists, attends and illuminates our experience.

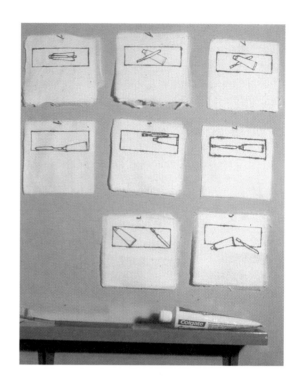

Eileen Neff is an artist and art critic who lives in Philadelphia. She is a regular contributor to Artforum, primarily reviewing Philadelphia-area work, and she recently completed a comprehensive essay for the retrospective exhibition of William Anastasi. Her artwork has been seen at the Philadelphia Museum of Art, the Institute of Contemporary Art, Philadelphia, and Artist's Space, New York. She teaches at the University of the Arts and Drexel University.

1 A cherry orchard grew on the site where Eastern State Penitentiary was built. Even in Europe, the prison was commonly known as Cherry Hill.

2 As one of many examples in literature, Thomas Mann's short stories explore the often difficult relationship between the artist and society. In the preface to *Stories of Three Decades,* Mann describes how for the title character of "Felix Krull," "the element of the unreal and illusional passes frankly over into the criminal." The brilliant, disturbed mind of Dostoyevsky's Raskolnikov in *Crime and Punishment* is another, related portrayal of the artist crossing this line.

3 Some of the interviews were recorded at Holmesburg Prison.

4 All quotations and historical facts about Cherry Hill not otherwise referenced are from Norman Johnston with Kenneth Finkel and Jeffrey A. Cohen, *Eastern State Penitentiary: Crucible of Good Intentions,* Philadelphia: Philadelphia Museum of Art for the Eastern Penitentiary Task Force of the Preservation Coalition of Greater Philadelphia, 1994.

5 from Healing in Time, p.27, Catalog essay from Culture in Action, Seattle: Bay Press, 1995.

Prisons and Other Visions of Criminal Justice

Russ Immarigeon

The most profound horror of prison lives in the day-to-day banal occurrences that turn days into months, and months into years, and years into decades. Prison is a second-by-second assault on the soul, a day-to-day degradation of the self, an oppressive steel and brick umbrella that transforms seconds into hours and hours into days. While a person is locked away in distant netherworlds, time seems to stand still; but it doesn't, of course. Children left outside grow into adulthood, often having children of their own. Once loving relationships wither into yesterday's dust. Relatives die, their loss mourned in silent loneliness. Times, temperaments, mores change, and the caged move to outdated rhythms.

Mumia Abu-Jamal
Death Row Inmate and Journalist
Philadelphia, Pennsylvania[2]

"THE PRACTICE OF LOCKING UP HUMAN BEINGS IN CONDITIONS OF CAPTIVITY CHALLENGES SOME OF THE BASIC PRINCIPLES OF HUMANITY. FOR THAT REASON ONE SHOULD BE PREPARED TO ASK FIRST-ORDER QUESTIONS. WHY DO WE HAVE PRISONS? WHAT ARE THEY MEANT TO ACHIEVE? DOES EVERYONE WHO IS IN PRISON NOW HAVE TO BE THERE? ARE THERE OTHER WAYS OF DEALING WITH PEOPLE WHO BREAK THE ACCEPTED NORMS OF SOCIETY?"

Andrew Coyle
Governor, Brixton Prison
London, England [1]

more than one and a half million American men and women are now confined in police lockups, county jails, and state and federal prisons across the United States. But Americans rarely ask about what happens in jails and prisons across the country. They rarely ask how they might experience imprisonment themselves, or, most importantly, how they would like to be treated if they broke the law and faced the prospect of time behind bars. Nor do they ask how they would like their sons or daughters, relatives or friends treated if they broke the law. What would they like their lives behind bars to be like? Would they think that their imprisonment was just? Would they think that something else less drastic, less severe than incarceration would have sufficed as a penalty, as a means of showing personal responsibility, as a method of "making amends" for the damage done, or as a way to repair the harm inflicted? These are first-order questions left woefully unattended in current debates over crime and justice.

A BRIEF HISTORY

Shortly after visiting Eastern State Penitentiary in 1831, Alexis de Tocqueville wrote his sister that Philadelphia was "infatuated ... with the penitentiary system." Eastern State Penitentiary was the product of Quaker-inspired efforts to replace the brutalities of corporal and capital punishments with a penitentiary regime that isolated criminals, keeping them away from other prisoners while engaging them in work and religious study in the solitude of their cells.

Befitting the purposeful founding vision of Eastern State Penitentiary, Samuel R. Wood, the institution's first warden, meticulously recorded many details about each of the initial cohort of prisoners, including criminal offense, age, race, gender, disciplinary infractions, general health, and so forth. But the readiness of Philadelphia courts to send offenders to the penitentiary soon started to overwhelm its ability to carry out its program. By September 1835, six years after the prison had received its first inmate, Eastern State Penitentiary had received 300 prisoners. In the next few months, a swell of prisoners was received, boosting the prison's population to 360 men and women. "The bloom was off the experiment," one historian has observed, "and the warden and the physician no longer had sufficient time to record in detail the ailments, idiosyncrasies, and minor infractions committed by their charges."[3]

Despite its reformist intentions, Eastern State Penitentiary soon received

further criticism. In 1842, Charles Dickens, then on a tour of North America, visited the prison, spoke with many of its prisoners, and condemned the entire Philadelphia experiment: "The system here is rigid, strict, and hopeless solitary confinement," he wrote in American Notes. "I believe it, in its effect, to be cruel and wrong."

"In its intention," Dickens continued, "I am well convinced that it is kind, humane, and meant for reformation; but I am persuaded that those who devised this system of Prison Discipline, and those benevolent gentlemen who carry it into execution, do not know what it is that they are doing. I believe that very few men are capable of estimating the immense amount of torture and agony which this dreadful punishment, prolonged for years, inflicts upon the sufferers; and in guessing at it myself, and in reasoning from what I have seen written upon their faces, and what to my certain knowledge they feel within, I am only the more convinced that there is a depth of terrible endurance in it which none but the sufferers themselves can fathom, and which no man has a right to inflict upon his fellow creature."[4]

Eastern State Penitentiary, designed by noted nineteenth-century architect John Haviland, was a marvel in many ways. In the 1990s, a visitor walking through the original cellblocks of Eastern State sees broad corridors, expansive archways, and a flood of sunlight that shines upon the prison's cracked and decaying walls. Nearly 25 years have passed since Eastern State closed in 1971. Weakened by time and nature and marred by cell blocks built over the years as its prisoner population grew ever larger, the prison is falling apart. Stepping over the dust of walls that prisoners once pressed

against, ducking and maneuvering up stair-
cases that were once the work route of
prison guards, a visitor to Eastern State
must wonder what went on in this place
for so many years.

How should men and women and
their communities and governments respond
to fellow citizens who have broken laws,
stolen property, or injured or killed people?
For much of the past two centuries, a mixture of rehabilitation and retribution guided
formal justice systems in the United States.
But the relationship between rehabilitation
and retributivism has always been uneasy.
Shortly after Eastern State Penitentiary
opened, opposition arose from others seeking a still more humane alternative. One
emerging alternative was probation, which
appeared in the 1840s; another was parole,
which came about in the 1890s. Throughout
the twentieth century, prison administrators
tried to operate model facilities. Prison
gardens, for instance, were developed to
engage prisoners in constructive activity
and to improve the image of the penitentiary
within the larger community. In the 1970s,
articles claiming that rehabilitation programs
were not effective in reducing recidivism
paved the way for the retrenchment of political support for such programs. Anti-prison
activists in this period also argued that prisoners were being held in prisons too long
and that black prisoners were being incarcerated more frequently and for longer
periods than white offenders. Collectively,
these forces, and society's heightened
awareness of crime and violence, created—
not always intentionally—fertile ground for
the greater use of imprisonment. Throughout
it all, prisons were securing their station as
the bedrock of criminal justice.

OUR PRISON CRISIS

Criminal justice policymaking has
become politicized in a way that seriously
jeopardizes our ability to make rational
choices. The major crisis with the use of
prisons today may be less that they are
overcrowded or they have too few treatment
programs, but rather that we, as a culture,
as a nation, have lost the ability to think
about the use of imprisonment in a manner
befitting a civilized democracy.

Crime policy in the 1990s is a con-
test to see who is toughest, who can establish longer sentences, who can execute
more people most quickly. In an era when
conversations about crime focus mainly on
mandatory sentences, longer sentences,
"three strikes and you're out" sentences and
death sentences, there is little likelihood that
the United States will discontinue policies
and practices that have tripled the country's
penal population in the past decade.
Although there is much political discourse
about making the offender accountable,
crime policy debate is really about punishing
or inflicting harm on people.

Prison policy in the 1990s is
increasingly centered on removing the few
tools that prison systems need to help
offenders build a better life for themselves,
for their families, and for their communities.
College education programs, for instance,
have virtually been eliminated, even though
these programs have shown consistently
positive results.[5] Increasingly, the level of
educational instruction offered within jails
and prisons has been reduced, assuring that
offenders will not be able to compete legiti-
mately with others in the free-world market-
place beyond the prison gates. Substance
abuse programs are frightfully scarce, and

even recreational activities, such as weight-lifting, which give offenders an opportunity to manifest pride and dignity, are being abolished. Some opponents of prison reform even protest family visits. Recently, Alabama has renewed programs of "purposeless work," such as chain gangs and breaking rocks, that were deemed inappropriate 125 years ago by prison professionals at the First National Conference on Penitentiary Reform, held in Cincinnati, Ohio, in 1870.

Litigation has been an important tool for addressing harsh prison conditions and overcrowded prison systems. In the 1960s and 1970s, a prisoner rights movement sprung up, demanding humane living conditions and professional treatment. Prisoners' rights cases involved a wide variety of concerns, from due process issues to overall prison conditions. Foremost, prisoners' rights law has evolved as an essential part of the civil and constitutional process of standards-setting in these institutions. As one federal judge notes, cases come about because no one else has taken them on and conditions were unlikely to change unless courts reviewed them.[6] In January 1995, the ACLU's National Prison Project reported that federal and state courts have ruled prison systems unconstitutional, in part or in whole, in 39 states plus the District of Columbia, Puerto Rico, and the Virgin Islands.[7]

Prison officials, often curiously left out of these debates, frequently find litigation strategies helpful to their work. Norval Morris, former Dean of The University of Chicago Law School, has observed that "when one talks, out of hours, with the superintendents and wardens of prisons and jails who are the defendants in these cases,

one finds that though these cases are demanding of their time and energy, the superintendents and wardens are appreciative that they are a powerful weapon against the politicians of their administrations, and the politicians of their legislatures, who tend to deny corrections the resources necessary to fulfill its mission."[8] Indeed, prison wardens in California, Delaware, Florida, Illinois, Michigan, Ohio, Pennsylvania, and Texas reported in a recent survey that political leaders in the U.S. Congress are offering "crime control measures" (more prisons, more death penalty statutes) that are least likely to increase public safety. Prison wardens want a more balanced approach that includes fewer mandatory sentences, more drug treatment programs, and the expansion of literacy and education programs.[9]

In the mid-1990s, however, American criminal justice is increasingly captive to expressions of a punitive justice based on anger and outrage, rather than realistic policies based on experience and practice. But relying on the criminal justice system, some scholars say, may itself be ineffective. According to highly regarded criminologists Michael R. Gottfredson and Travis Hirschi, reliance on the criminal justice system is short-sighted: "The formal criminal justice system, with its procedural guarantees, its necessarily after-the-fact identification of and response to crime, its array of penalties removed in time and character from the acts with which it is concerned, and its ties to politics and publicity, will be unable to deal with crime and criminals."[10]

Police officers, probation and parole agents, judges, prosecutors and defense attorneys, community-based service providers, and correctional staff consume an exorbitant amount of public fiscal resources. Studies in several states, including California, Maryland, and Washington, D.C., suggest that incarcerating offenders for longer periods of time is stripping these states' capacity to provide for an adequate level of public education for children and young people. Many rural and small communities are learning that they cannot pursue capital punishment because death penalty cases deplete local budgets. But few states conduct meaningful fiscal impact statements to assess the potential cost of specific legislation or policy shifts or to establish policy initiates that are associated with the ability to actually provide promised services.

MYTH AND MISDIRECTION

Criminal justice policy is viewed with confusion by many people in the United States. Political scientist Kathryn Gaubatz Taylor recently interviewed a cross-section of Americans and found that "public opinion about crime is not a seamless web. The public that wants a greater use of incarceration also believes that our prisons are not particularly effective; the public that calls for harsher courts also believes that an attack on socioeconomic problems would do more to reduce crime."[11]

Myths about criminal justice are many.[12] Crime is at an all-time high. We don't lock up enough offenders. Prisons reduce crime. Longer sentences are more effective. The public wants more criminals imprisoned. Larger police forces reduce crime. We need more prison space for violent offenders. Reality, however, suggests otherwise. The public, for example, is very concerned about crime. But those less

directly affected by crime are most fearful. And although the public wants something done about crime, opinion polls have consistently shown that Americans support rehabilitation, helping offenders redirect their lives, and helping them become good citizens. When people are given choices about how to treat offenders, they are more likely to choose community service or restitution, where offenders give something back to victims and the community, than incarceration, which is a costly method of warehousing prisoners and wasting scarce public funds.[13] Studies show that people even support these options for offenders convicted of some violent offenses.[14]

Misdirections are also plentiful. Recently, the governor of New York State issued an executive order forbidding prisoners convicted of violent offenses to participate in work release programs. This is a politically popular approach in the current penal climate.[15] Again, the reality is otherwise.

The Correctional Association of New York, one of the nation's oldest nongovernmental organizations fighting for improvements in the administration of criminal justice, notes the following:

In May 1994, Thomas Coughlin, then Commissioner of New York's prison system, testified before the Senate Crime Victims, Crime, and Corrections Committee that in the previous three years about 1,000 participants in New York's work release program had originally been convicted of a crime involving a death. "When those 1,000 went out on work release," the Commissioner stated, "eleven of them—I repeat, eleven—were arrested again. Not one was arrested for murder, but one for trespass. Not one was arrested for manslaughter, but one for hindering prosecution. Not one was arrested for criminally negligent homicide, but three were arrested for drug possession." Only 1.1% of these offenders were rearrested, and almost half of those were charged with only minor breaches of the law. Similarly, the Division of Parole records show that parolees convicted of the most serious offenses have the lowest rate of revocation, 14.8%. This rate compares with 27.6% for people convicted of drug crimes and 38% for property offenders.[16]

It is also noteworthy that research consistently shows that sentencing options less restrictive than incarceration are often cost-effective while increasing public safety. Researchers have found, for instance, that just paying a small fine or some restitution reduces offenders' likelihood of reoffending.[17] Research also shows that offenders who participate in work release or prison furlough programs have significantly lower rates of recidivism than offenders who are released directly into the community at the end of their sentence without ameliorative, community reintegration experiences and services.[18]

INSTEAD OF IMPRISONMENT

In the mid-1970s, the Prison Research Education Action Project, a citizen-based reform group, urged the near abolition of prisons. They suggested that instead of prisons we should pursue a "caring community" approach that empowered prisoners to take responsibility for their actions and behavior; developed a network of health, educational, vocational, residential, counseling, and legal services in the community; and established victim-assistance, restitution, and compensation programs.[19] Twenty years ago, courts would impose probation sentences with special conditions, such as substance abuse counseling, literacy classes, and job training as alternatives to incarceration. Today, alternatives to prison are often fashioned as retributive rather than rehabilitative sanctions.

Intermediate sanctions, such as day-fines and community service, are being widely used across the country. Intermediate sanctions are penalties that are considered less onerous than prison but more restrictive than simple probation. The primary principle behind intermediate sanctions is the need to develop rational and effective sentencing practices and policies. "Imprisonment is used excessively," write two leading advocates of intermediate sanctions, "probation is used even more excessively; between the two is a near-vacuum of purposive and enforced punishments."[20]

Intermediate Sanctions Include:

Fines: Fines are used more widely in the United States than is often recognized and recent research shows that they are surprisingly effective. Fines are usually given to offenders as established by law, with little attention given the economic status of the offender. Fines are used more routinely in Western Europe and Scandinavia, particularly as alternatives to prison.[21]

Day Fines: Day fines are established according to the offender's economic status. Fixed rate fines can be inequitable; for instance, a $50 fine is greater for someone making $10,000 a year than it is for someone making $100,000 a year. Day fines are prorated. Usually, they are imposed through a two-step process. First, judges give offenders a certain number of units based on the severity of the offense, regardless of the offender's economic circumstances. Second, the value of each fine unit is calculated in relationship to the offender's daily wage. One figure is multiplied by the other to determine the day-fine amount.[22]

Restitution: Restitution is usually a financial payment by the offender directly to the victim for property lost or for harm inflicted. In some cases, the amount of restitution approximates the value of the property stolen or destroyed. In other cases, where the offender does not have the means to pay, partial restitution may be imposed.[23]

Community Service: Community service is unpaid work done by the offender either for the victim or for the community. If the victim desires, the offender can mow lawns, cut wood, and do similar work that helps repay victims for their losses. Offenders may be sentenced to work for private, non-profit, or governmental agencies to repay the community for their actions. In England and Wales, a limit is set on the number of hours of community service work that can be meted out to individual offenders. In the United States, there is no limit and, in general, no guidelines have been established to apply length or type of work assignments with the nature or number of offenses committed. In New York City, relatively short periods of community service have been used effectively to reduce jail time without risking public safety.[24]

Intensive Supervision Probation and Parole: Intensive supervision allows probation and parole officers more time to give focused attention to specific offenders. Usually, officers are given a reduced caseload (often 20 to 25 cases per officer, instead of the 80 to 120 cases often handled by many officers). This gives officers the chance to meet with, work together with, and monitor offenders in a more detailed manner. When used for cases that require more attention, intensive supervision allows officers to provide the services that are necessary to address the offender deficits and problems.[25]

Home confinement with electronic monitoring, day reporting centers, and boot camps are other intermediate sanctions widely used.[26]

AN AGENDA FOR REFORM

A new paradigm of principles may be necessary to guide our criminal justice system. A long-time prison observer recently summed up the status quo for prisons in the United States: they will be a fixture in this country for a long time; they are authoritarian communities; programs are the only hope for prisoners; and prisoners treated with hate will become brutal, but prisoners given civility (much as we would expect civility in the way people meet us) "will take on the characteristics of civility in a community that places a value on civility."[27]

Several years ago, The Sentencing Project, a public interest group located in Washington D.C., organized "A Campaign for an Effective Crime Policy," a non-partisan movement of more than 1,400 criminal justice professionals, elected officials, and community leaders in 50 states seeking to depoliticize crime policy and to implement realistic and effective crime policies. "To rebuild the economic and social vitality of our nation's cities," a policy statement suggests, "we must deal more effectively with crime. Public and private resources can be targeted more efficiently to implement crime prevention and reduction measures, to deal appropriately with offenders and victims, and to build community participation in creating solutions to crime problems."[28]

The Campaign for an Effective Crime Policy offers some sound suggestions: establish a National Crime Commission to assess what we have learned in the past twenty years about the causes, prevention, and reduction of crime and about the administration and application of criminal justice interventions; provide substance abuse treatment for all offenders who require it; give greater attention to crime prevention programs such as early childhood intervention, family support programs, mental health services, violence prevention training, and mediation programs; and rely more on alternatives to incarceration such as restitution, fines, intensive supervision, community service, residential treatment, and other options that have proven more effective than incarceration.[29]

A rational and effective response to crime, the group argues, would address social and economic conditions conducive to criminality, repair the damage done by crime, provide compensation or restitution to crime victims, enable offenders to take responsibility for their actions, and help build a stronger sense of community. In brief, it hopes to mobilize the political will to address the root causes of crime by identifying policies that are sensible (rather than simply tough-sounding) and restorative (rather than destructive).

"According to restorative justice," writes Howard Zehr, a historian and leading proponent of this approach, "crime violates people and relationships; justice aims to identify needs and obligations so that things can be made right; justice encourages dialogue and mutual agreement, gives victims and offenders central roles, and is judged by the extent to which responsibilities are assumed, needs are met, and healing of individuals and relationships is encouraged."[30]

This is a visionary approach, quite different in its appeal from the rhetoric of "three strikes and you're out," but the translation of restorative justice principles into practice is already underway. At least three avenues of redress have been proposed and put into practice in recent years.

Victim-Offender Mediation: Victim-offender mediation involves a meeting between offenders and their victims in the company of a third-party facilitator. Victim-offender mediation theory suggests that crime is a conflict between victims and offenders that has been dominated by state or system interests, rather than victim or offender interests. Victim-offender mediation is a way to return criminal conflicts to victims and offenders to resolve. Victim-offender meetings, which are voluntary, allow victims and offenders to express their feelings about what has occurred. Victims can learn why they were victimized. Offenders can learn how their actions affected the victims. Victims and offenders can also develop a mutually agreeable sentencing plan, including community service or restitution. The primary purpose of these meetings is to reconcile and to repair the damage done. Victim-offender mediation meetings have been conducted in over 200 North American communities.

Restorative Community Justice: Restorative community justice, according to the National Organization of Victim Assistance, involves bringing all offenders to account through punishment and reparation to both the victims and the communities they hurt by committing criminal offenses. Among the principals central to this approach are: (a) criminal justice should address victims as well as offenders; (b) communities should implement behavioral standards established by government through criminal laws; (c) community institutions should be strengthened through the democratic enforcement of these laws; (d) harmonious relationships between parties are improved through justice that is imposed quickly, skillfully, and locally; (e) offenders, victims, and communities all have responsibilities; and (f) justice should restore individual dignity and community bonds. A program for creating restorative community justice would include community policing, community prosecution, community courts, and community corrections.[31]

Family Group Conferences: A family group conference is a mediative structure within which extended family members are included in and empowered by the process of making decisions about where children with absent or abusive parents are placed or about what sanctions should be imposed upon young people who have broken the law. In 1989, New Zealand implemented legislation that gives presumptive authority for such an approach in all care and protection and most juvenile offending cases. In brief, the practice assumes that family members know more about each other and are more able than professionals to offer continuous care and services to each other. In New Zealand, when an arrest or referral is made to the appropriate court, an independent coordinator investigates the background of the case, including the current concern, identifies and locates extended family members, contacts relevant social service and mental health professionals, and convenes a family group conference. In the first stage of this conference, all parties are brought together to be informed about the situation. In many cases, family members do not know what has been happening, and they welcome the new information. Professionals often contribute useful information about particular problems. They are not there to assume responsibility for intervening; rather,

responsibility is for the family to claim. Accordingly, professionals are viewed as helping, not meddling. Once all information has been shared, the extended family retreats to a private setting where they discuss matters and develop a placement or sanctioning plan. The coordinator later helps them write up this plan for the court. In New Zealand, over 90 percent of these plans are accepted by the judiciary. Family group conferences have effectively diverted offenders from court and detention, stressed offender accountability, included victims, strengthened families, and increased awareness of the utility of culturally sensitive interventions.[32]

The introduction of restorative justice concepts to public and political debate about what can be done with a retributive justice system that relies on measures such as arrest, conviction, supervision, incarceration, and even execution is not likely to occur unless there is either new leadership among criminal justice policy makers or a groundswell of community (i.e., political constituent) support for approaching crime and victimization in a new way.

"Public opinion can be influenced by leadership," one prison authority noted several years ago, "but there has to be a message, a plan, a policy that is clearly articulated and readily understood. And even if a message, a plan, or policy is clearly articulated, one cannot depend on the political process to develop it, and carry out its implementation. Implementation is dependent on a coalition of strong professional groups, civic organizations and independent groups who can work together within the political process without being controlled by it."[33]

Criminal justice reform in the United States is at a crossroads. Policy can be based on punitive measures ranging from the use of electronic monitoring devices to the expansion of "super-max" prisons. Or, policy can be determined by restorative justice principles and practice, a method of "repairing the damage" done by crime that is increasingly championed by victim groups, religion-based organizations, and prisoner rights agencies.

Prison policy will change, William G. Nagel said some years ago, only when there is the political will to do so.[34] It is instructive to consider the case of changes occurring in South Africa. Until recently, South Africa and the United States had the highest rates of incarceration in the world. Violence was prevalent, and capital punishment was used in both countries. But South Africa has instituted rapid and significant policy changes. Nelson Mandela, who was a political prisoner while the United States tripled its prison population, is now President of South Africa. Black South Africans now vote. Apartheid no longer exists. Recently, the South African Supreme Court abolished capital punishment, a remarkable shift in policy, given that South Africa once executed more people than any other nation. South Africa is also completely revamping its juvenile justice system to divert offenders from courts and confinement, to ensure culturally sensitive processes, to make greater use of conflict resolution procedures, to increase victim and offender involvement in the judicial process, and to establish sentences that transform offenders rather than stigmatize them.

South Africa demonstrates the ability of a nation to radically change its course. Restorative justice provides a rationale for such a change. In the United States, some first-order questions remain especially timely for citizens and political leaders alike: Why do we continue to build prisons? What are they meant to achieve? What do they actually achieve? Does sending so many offenders to prison really benefit victims, offenders, and communities? And, are there other ways of dealing with people who break the our laws? These are important questions for us all.

Russ Immarigeon is a freelance writer. For twenty years, he has worked on criminal justice and corrections issues as a direct service provider, research evaluator, legislative analyst, community activist, and consultant to a variety of governmental and private agencies and associations. With Meda Chesney-Lind, he is co-author of Women's Prisons: Overcrowded and Overused, *published in 1992 by the National Council on Crime & Delinquency, and co-editor of the series, "Women, Crime and Criminology," published by the State University of New York Press. He lives in Hillsdale, New York.*

1 Andrew Coyle, *The Prisons We Deserve.* London: Harper Collins Publishers, 1994. p. 2.

2 Mumia Abu-Jamal, *Live from Death Row.* New York, NY: Addison-Wesley Publishing Co., 1995. p. 64-65.

3 Jacqueline Thibault, "'To Pave the Way to Penitence': Prisoners and Discipline at the Eastern State Penitentiary 1829-1835." The Pennsylvania Magazine of History and Biography, 56(2): 193, April 1982.

4 Charles Dickens, *American Notes: A Journey.* New York: Fromm International Publishing Corporation, 1985. p. 99.

5 See, generally, Miriam Williford, ed., *Higher Education in Prison: A Contradiction in Terms?.* Phoenix, AZ: The Oryx Press, 1994, or Howard S. Davidson, ed.,

Schooling in a "Total Institution": Critical Perspectives on Prison Education. Westport, CT: Bergin & Garvey, 1995.

6 Morris E. Lasker, *Forward.* In: Ira P. Robbins (editor), *Prisoners and the Law.* New York, NY: Clark Boardman Company, Ltd., 1985. p. xii.

7 The National Prison Project. Status Report: *State Prisons and the Courts.* Washington, DC: American Civil Liberties Union, 1995.

8 Norval Morris, *Forward.* In: Ira P. Robbins (editor), *Prisoners and the Law.* New York, NY: Clark Boardman Callaghan, 1994. p. xii.

9 This information was reported in a December 19, 1994 news release from the office of U.S. Senator Paul Simon (D-Illinois).

10 Michael R. Gottfredson and Travis Hirschi, "National Crime Control Policies." Society, 32(2): 34, January/ February 1995.

11 Kathryn Taylor Gaubatz, *Crime in the Public Mind.* Ann Arbor, MI: The University of Michigan Press, 1995. p. 2.

12 Four volumes that explore crime and crime policy myths are Harold E. Pepinsky and Paul Jesilow, *Myths that Cause Crime* (Cabin John, MD: Seven Locks Press, 1984); Kevin N. Wright, *The Great American Crime Myth* (Westport, CT: Greenwood Press, 1985); Victor E. Kappler, Mark Blumberg, and Gary W. Potter, *The Mythology of Crime and Criminal Justice* (Waveland Press, Inc., 1993); and Samuel Walker, *Sense and Nonsense about Crime and Drugs,* Third Edition (Belmont, CA: Wadsworth Publishing Company, 1994).

13 The Edna McConnell Clark Foundation has funded studies in Alabama, Delaware, Maine and Pennsylvania that give citizens not only choices but rationales for sentencing options. See, for example, John Doble and Josh Klein, "Punishing Criminals - The Public's View: An Alabama Survey (1989)" and John Doble, Stephen Immerwahr, and Amy Richardson, "Punishing Criminals: The People of Delaware Consider the Options (1991)." These and other reports are available from The Edna McConnell Clark Foundation, 250 Park Ave, New York, NY 10017, (212) 986-7050.

14 The only survey that explores the use of non-incarcerative options for violent criminals is the British Crime Survey which found that citizens were willing to accept the use of community service orders, for instance, used for offenders convicted of certain violent offenses. Public attitudes on sentencing criminals in Australia, Canada, England and Wales, The Netherlands, and the United States are explored in Nigel Walker and Mike Hough, eds., *Public Attitudes in Sentencing: Surveys from Five Countries,* Gower Publishing Company, 1988.

15 David C. Anderson, former editorial page writer for The New York Times and The Wall Street Journal, writes about this environment in *Crime & The Politics of Hysteria: How the Willie Horton Story Changed American Justice* (Times Books, 1995). Willie Horton is the Massachusetts convict who brutally assaulted a middle-class Maryland couple while he was on furlough; Massachusetts Governor Michael Dukakis was running for President, at the time and Horton's crimes were used by Democrats and Republicans alike to frame the campaign's crime policy debate. "In an era of expressive justice." Anderson reflected recently, "crime control was no longer the point. The Willie Horton story aroused political self-protective instincts." Similarly, in *It's All the Rage: Crime and Culture* (Addison-Wesley, 1995), another journalist, Wendy Kaminer, concludes that crime control debates "have always been symbolized by imagery" rather than substance.

16 For further information, contact The Correctional Association of New York, 135 East 15th Street, New York, NY 10003, (212) 254-5700.

17 Margaret A. Gordon and Daniel Glaser, "The Use and Effects of Financial Penalties in Municipal Courts." Criminology, 29(4): 651-676, November 1991.

18 Ironically, given the Willie Horton episode, the best of these studies have been conducted by the Massachusetts Department of Corrections. See, for example, Daniel P. LeClair, *The Effect of Community Reintegration on Rates of Recidivism: A Statistical Overview of Data for the Years 1971 Through 1985.* Boston, MA: Massachusetts Department of Corrections, July 1988.

19 Fay Honey Knopp, et al. *Instead of Prisons: A Handbook for Abolitionists.* Syracuse, NY: Prison Research Education Action Project, 1976. p. 63.

20 Norval Morris and Michael Tonry, *Between Prison and Probation: Intermediate Punishments in a Rational Sentencing System.* New York: Oxford University Press, 1990. p. 3.

21 Sally T. Hillsman, "Fines and Day Fines." In: Norval Morris and Michael Tonry, eds., "Crime and Justice: An Annual Review." (Volume 12.) Chicago, IL: The University of Chicago Press, 1990. pp. 49-98.

22 Judith A. Greene, "Structuring Criminal Fines: Making an 'Intermediate Penalty' More Useful and Equitable." The Justice System Journal, 13(1): 37-50, Spring 1988.

23 Anne L. Schneider, *Deterrence and Juvenile Crime: Results from a National Policy Experiment.* New York, NY: Springer-Verlag, 1990.

24 Douglas Corry McDonald, *Punishment Without Walls.* New Brunswick, NJ: Rutgers University Press, 1986.

25 American Probation and Parole Association, *Restructuring Intensive Supervision Programs: Applying What Works.* Lexington, KY: APPA, 1994.

26 For a general up-to-date assessment of intermediate sanctions, see Michael Tonry and Kate Hamilton, eds., *Intermediate Sanctions in Overcrowded Times* (Northeastern University Press, 1995). For other treatments of these penalties, see James M. Bryne, Arthur J. Lurgio, and Joan Petersilia, eds., *Smart Sentencing: The Emergence of Intermediate Sanctions* (Sage Publications, 1992); Malcolm Davies, *Punishing Criminals: Developing Community-Based Intermediate Sanctions* (Greenwood Press, 1993); Charles B. Fields, ed., *Innovative Trends and Specialized Strategies in Community-Based Corrections* (Garland Publishing, Inc., 1994); and John Ortiz Smykla and William L. Selke, eds., *Intermediate Sanctions: Sentencing in the 1990s* (Anderson Publishing Co., 1995).

27 John P. Conrad, *"What Do the Underserving Deserve?" The Pains of Imprisonment,* edited by Robert Johnson and Hans Toch. Bverly Hills, CA: Sage Publications, 1982, p. 328.

28 For further information, contact Beth Carter, National Coordinator, Campaign for an Effective Crime Policy, 918 F Street, N.W., Suite 505, Washington, D.C. 20004, (202) 628-1903.

29 Some of these proposals are already influential. Recently, President Clinton announced six nominees to a National Commission on Crime Control and Prevention, established by last year's federal crime bill. Other members will soon be named by the President and by Congressional leaders. The Committee will report its findings in two years on successful crime control programs, the causes of substance abuse and other factors contributing to crime, and recommendations for improving the criminal justice system.

30 Howard Zehr, *Changing Lenses: A New Focus for Crime and Justice.* Scottsdale, PA: Herald Press, 1990. p. 211.

31 Marlene A. Young, *Restorative Community Justice: A Call to Action.* Washington, DC: National Organization of Victim Assistance, 1995.

32 Richard Wilcox, et al., *Family Decision Making/ Family Group Conferences: Practitioners' Views.* Lower Hutt, New Zealand: Practitioners' Publishing; Gabrielle M. Maxwell and Allison Morris, *Family, Victims and Culture: Youth Justice in New Zealand.* Wellington, New Zealand: Social policy Agency and Institute of Criminology, Victoria University of Wellington, 1993.

33 Allen Breed, *The State of Corrections Today: A Triumph of Pluralistic Ignorance.* New York, NY: The Edna McConnell Clark Foundation, n.d. p. 8.

34 William G. Nagel, *The New Red Barn: A Critical Look at the Modern American Prison.* New York, NY: Walker and Company, 1973.

Photo by Todd Gilens

ARTISTS' BIOGRAPHIES

JOHN J. ABNER

Born in Philadelphia, Pennsylvania, 1956.
Philadelphia Community College, 1982-86.
Fleisher Art Memorial, Philadelphia, 1986-88.
Tyler School of Art, Philadelphia, 1988- present.

SELECTED GROUP EXHIBITIONS

1994 "Women and Children First,"
The Esther M. Klein Gallery, Philadelphia.

1994 Intermedia Arts Gallery, Minneapolis, Minnesota.

1993 "High Flying," Institute of Contemporary Art,
Philadelphia.

1992 Temple University Gallery, Philadelphia.

BETH B

Born in New York, New York, 1955.
San Diego State University, 1972.
University of California, Irvine, 1973.
School of Visual Arts, New York, BFA, 1976.

VIDEO SHORTS AND DOCUMENTARIES

1994 "High Heel Nights." With Keith Levy, Mikel Gorski.
Arte TV, France. 10 mins.

1993 "Under Lock and Key." With Nan Golden, Robbie Macauley.
Wexner Center for the Arts, Columbus, Ohio. 30 mins.

1992 "Amnesia." Television Spot for "Trans-Voices" Project.
The Whitney Museum of American Art, New York and
The American Center, Paris. 1 min.

1991 "Stigmata." Electronic Arts Intermix, New York. 40 mins.

"Thanatopsis." With Lydia Lunch. Electronic Arts Intermix,
New York. 11 mins.

1989 "Belladonna." With Jonas Mekas. Sebastian Mekas
Electronic Arts Intermix. 13 mins.

FILMS

1993 "Two Small Bodies." Starring Fred Ward, Suzi Amis.
Castle Hill Productions. ZDF and Arte TV. 85 mins.

1987 "Salvation!" Starring Viggo Mortensen, Exene
Cervenka, Stephen McHattie. Circle Releasing. 87 mins.

1983 "Vortex." Starring James Russo, Lydia Lunch.
First Run Features. 85 mins.

1981 "The Trap Door." Starring Jack Smith.
First Run Features. 80 mins.

1979 "The Offenders." Starring John Lurie, Lydia Lunch.
First Run Features. 90 mins.

1978 "Black Box." Starring Lydia Lunch.
First Run Features. 25 mins.

1978 "Letters to Dad." Starring Kiki Smith, Tom Otterness,
John Ahearn. First Run Features. 15 mins.

1978 "G-Man." Starring Bill Rice and Marcia Resnick.
First Run Features. 30 mins.

SELECTED INDIVIDUAL EXHIBITIONS

1995 "Inside Out," Jose Freire Gallery, New York and
Temple Gallery, Philadelphia.

"Trophies," PPOW, Sculpture exhibition, New York.

1994 "Violence/Business," Photographic Compositions,
Neue Gesellschaft fur bildende Kunst, Curated by Frank
Wagner, Berlin, Germany.

"Under Lock and Key and Amnesia Installations," Santa
Monica Museum of Art, Santa Monica, California (also
Wexner Center for the Arts, Columbus, Ohio, 1993).

"Amnesia," New Langton Arts, San Francisco, California.

"Under Lock and Key," International Center of Photography,
New York.

1992 "Stigmata, Thanatopsis, Belladonna," Museum of
Modern Art, New York (Also at the Roxy Theater, New
Langton Arts and Pacific Film Archives, San Francisco).

"Days of Hope," Public Arts Project, installation of 50 newspaper
dispensers distributing bilingual newspaper throughout Manhattan.

"Salvation!, Thanatopsis, Stigmata, Belladonna," Danish Film
Institute, Copenhagen, Denmark (and 12 cities Germany and
Holland, 1991).

1991 "Thanatopsis and American Nightmare," Hallwalls,
Buffalo, New York.

"Belladonna and Thanatopsis," The Kitchen, New York.

1990 "Poster Series: Surgeon General's Warning," Creative Time Citywide, New York.

1989 "Belladonna," with the Ida Applebroog Exhibition, Ronald Feldman Fine Arts, New York.

SELECTED GROUP EXHIBITIONS

1992 *The Exploding Valentine,* "Belladonna," The Kitchen, New York.

Trans Voices, "Amnesia," The American Center, Paris.

1991 "1991 Biennial Exhibition," Whitney Museum of American Art, New York. Catalogue.

"Selections from the Circulating Library." Museum of Modern Art. Curated by Barbara London. (Also in 1990).

"Traveling Show," Curated by Christine Van Assche, Centre Georges Pompidou, Paris.

1990 New Works; "Belladonna." American Film Institute Video Festival, Los Angeles.

Moving Image Exhibition, "Belladonna," Museo Nacional Centro de Arte Reina Sofia, Madrid Biennale, Spain.

SELECTED BIBLIOGRAPHY

Knight, Christopher. "Beth B's 'Amnesia' Burns into Our Memory." Calendar Section. *Los Angles Times* (29 March 1994).

James, Caryn. "Did She or Didn't She? Commit Murder, That is. *New York Times* (15 April 1994).

Catlin, Chad. "The "B" Side." *Venice Magazine* (April 1994).

Constable, Leslie. "Veneer of Normalcy Broken." *The Columbus* (1 August 1993).

McCormick, Carlo. "High Art." *High Times* (February 1991).

Heartney, Eleanor. "Ida Applebroog and Beth B at Feldman." *Art in America* (January 1990).

Rickey, Carrie. "A Stylish and Wicked Satire of Televangelism." *The Philadelphia Inquirer* (17 July 1987).

Pulleine, Tim. "The Salvation of Beth B." *The London Times* (August 1987).

Gelmis. "From Antonioni to the Bs." *Newsday* (1 October 1982).

Rose, Frank. "Welcome to the Modern World." *Esquire Magazine* (April 1981)

JONATHAN BOROFSKY

Born in Boston, Massachusetts, 1942.
Carnegie Mellon University, Pittsburgh, Pennsylvania, BFA, 1964.
Ecole de Fontainebleu, France, 1964.
Yale School of Art and Architecture, New Haven, Connecticut, MFA, 1966.

SELECTED INDIVIDUAL EXHIBITIONS

1995 "Man With a Heart," Grand Central Terminal, New York.

Paula Cooper Gallery, New York. (Also in 1993, 1991, 1990, 1988, 1983, 1980, 1979, 1976, 1975).

1990 "Jonathan Borofsky: Dessins," Galerie Yvon Lambert, Paris. (Also in 1987)

1987 Tokyo Metropolitan Museum. Traveled to the Museum of Modern Art, Shiga. Catalogue with text by Mark Rosenthal. Galerie Watari, Tokyo. (Also in 1984)

1984 "Jonathan Borofsky," Philadelphia Museum of Art. Traveled to Whitney Museum of American Art, New York; University Art Museum, Berkeley; Walker Art Center, Minneapolis; The Corcoran Gallery of Art, Washington, DC; Los Angeles Museum of Contemporary Art. Catalogue with text by Mark Rosenthal and Richard Marshall.

1983 "Jonathan Borofsky: Zeichnungen 1960-1983," Kunstmuseum Basel, Basel, Switzerland. Traveled to Stadtisches Kunstmuseum Bonn, Bonn, West Germany; Kunstverein in Hamburg; Kunsthalle Bielefeld, Bielefield, West Germany; Mannheimer Kunstverein, Manheim West Germany; Moderna Museet, Stockholm, Sweden.

1982 Museum Boymans-Van Beuningen, Rotterdam, The Netherlands.

1981 Contemporary Arts Museum, Houston, Texas.

1973 Artists Space, New York.

SELECTED GROUP EXHIBITIONS

1995 "Critiques of Pure Abstraction," Blaffer Gallery, University of Houston, Houston. Traveling through 1997.

1994 "From Minimal to Conceptual Art: Works from the Dorothy and Herbert Vogel Collection," National Gallery of Art, Washington DC.

1993 "American Art in the 20th Century: Painting and Sculpture," Martin-Gropius-Bau, Berlin.
Traveled to Royal Academy of Arts, London.

1992 "Allegories of Modernism: Contemporary Drawing," The Museum of Modern Art, New York.

"Documenta IX," Museum Fridericianum, Kassel, West Germany. Also "Documenta VII" in 1982.

1991 "Metropolis," Martin-Gropius-Bau, Berlin.

1990 "The Readymade Boomerang: Certain Relations in 20th Century Art," Eighth Biennial of Sydney, Art Gallery of New South Wales, Sydney, Australia. Catalogue.

1987 "A Century of Modern Sculpture:
Patsy and Raymond Nasher Collection," Dallas Museum of Art, Dallas. Traveled to the National Gallery of Art, Washington DC.

1985 "18th Biennial de São Paulo," São Paulo, Brazil.

1984 "An International Survey of Recent Painting and Sculpture," The Museum of Modern Art, New York.

1982 "Zeitgeist," Martin-Gropius-Bau, Berlin.

1979 "Biennial Exhibition," Whitney Museum of American Art, New York. Also in 1981 and 1983.

SELECTED BIBLIOGRAPHY

Borofsky, Jonathan. "Dreams." *The Paris Review* (Winter 1981).

Zimmer, William. "Portrait of the Artist as a One-Man World." *The New York Times* (20 January 1985).

Kuspit, Donald. "Jonathan Borofsky." *Artforum* (Summer 1990): 160.

Shaffner, Ingrid. "Jonathan Borofsky." *Artscribe* (Summer 1990): 80-81.

"A Drawing Page by Jonathan Borofsky." *Artforum* (December 1990): 89.

Di Pietrantonio, Giacinto. "Jonathan Borofsky; Portikus." *FlashArt* (October 1991): 146-148.

Larson, Kay. "Artists the Critics are Watching: Jonathan Borofsky Counting to a Billion." *Artnews* (May 1991 [reprinted in November 1992]).

Upshaw, Reagen. "Jonathan Borofsky at Paula Cooper." (October 1993): 139.

Boettger, Susan. "Endless Columns: The Quest for Infinite Extension." *Sculpture* (January/February 1994): 28-33

JAMES CASEBERE

Born in Lansing, Michigan, 1953.
Minneapolis College of Art and Design, BFA, 1976.
Whitney Independent Study Program, New York, 1977.
California Institute of Art, MFA, Los Angeles, 1979.

SELECTED INDIVIDUAL EXHIBITIONS

1995 Michael Klein Gallery, New York (also in 1993, 1991 [Catalogue with text by Marge Goldwater], 1987).

1994 Galleria Galliani, Genoa, Italy.

"Prints and Collages," Richard Levy Gallery, Albequerque, New Mexico.

1991 Galerij Bruges La Morte, Bruges, Belgium.

"Model Fictions: The Photographs of James Casebere," Birmingham Museum of Art, Birmingham, Alabama.

"Station Projects" (with Tony Oursler), Kunststichting Kanaal, Kortrijk, Belgium.

1990 APAC, Center d'Art Contemporain, Nevers, France.

Galleria Fac-simile, Milan.

1989 "Tree Trunk with Broken Bungalo and Shotgun Houses." Neuberger Museum, State University of New York at Purchase. Catalogue with text by Marge Goldwater.

1987 "James Casebere and Barbara Ess," Interim Art, London.

1985 Minneapolis College of Art And Design.

1984 Sonnabend Gallery, New York. (Also in 1982).

1981 Franklin Furnace, New York.

1979 Artists Space, New York.

SELECTED GROUP EXHIBITIONS

1995 "Campo." Venice Biennale, Venice, Italy.

1994 "House Rules." Wexner Center for the Arts, Columbus, Ohio.

1993 "American Made: The New Still-Life," Isetan Museum of Art; Hokkaido Obihito Museum of Art, Japan. Traveled to the Royal College of Art, London. Catalogue with text by Patty Carroll.

1992 "More Than One Photography," Museum of Modern Art, New York.

1989 "32 Portraits: Photography in Art," The Hague, Contemporary Art Foundation, Amsterdam, Holland.

"The Photography of Invention: American Pictures of the 1980s," National Museum of American Art, Washington, DC. Traveled to the Walker Art Center, Minneapolis, Minnesota.

1985 "Biennial Exhibition," Whitney Museum of American Art, New York. Catalogue.

"In Plato's Cave," Marlborough Gallery, New York.

1983 Art Park, Lewiston, New York. Catalogue.

1982 "Tableaux: Nine Contemporary Sculptors," The Contemporary Art Center, Cincinnati, Ohio. Catalogue with text by Michael Klein.

SELECTED GRANTS AND AWARDS

1995 Solomon R. Guggenheim Fellowship.

1990 N.E.A., Visual Arts Fellowship. (Also in 1985, 1982).

1985 New York Foundation for the Arts Fellowship.

1982 New York State Council on the Arts; Visual Artists Sponsored Project Grant.

SELECTED BIBLIOGRAPHY

Conti, Viana. "James Casebere." *Flash Art* (March 1994): 78.

Anonymous. "James Casebere Silverprints." *The Paris Review* (Spring 1994): 229-235.

Hagen, Charles. "James Casebere." *The New York Times* (14 May 1993): C26.

Kalina, Richard. "James Casebere at Michael Klein." *Art in America* (October 1993): 127-128.

Lifson, Ben. "A Model Prisoner: James Casebere." *Artforum* (May 1993): 87-89.

Baker. Kenneth. "Art." *San Francisco Chronicle, Datebook* (magazine section) (23 August 1992): 45.

Handy, Ellen. "New York in Review." *Arts Magazine* (January 1992): 77.

Kimmelman, Michael. "Joys and Terrors on the Home Front. " *The New York Times* (27 September 1991): C1, C22.

Princenthal, Nancy. "James Casebere at Vrej Baghoomian." *Art in America* (June 1990): 170.

Jarmusch, Ann. "Casebere Show Lights Up Recesses of Mind." *San Diego Tribune* (26 October 1990): C1, C6.

MALCOLM COCHRAN

Born in Pittsburgh, Pennsylvania, 1948.
Cranbrook Academy of Art, Bloomfield Hills, Michigan, MFA, 1973.
Wesleyan University, Middletown, Connecticut, BA, 1971.

SELECTED INDIVIDUAL EXHIBITIONS

1994 "Field of Corn (with Osage Oranges)," commission for Art in Public Places Program, Dublin Arts Council, Dublin, Ohio.

1993 "The Difference Between Religion and a Relationship with Christ," commission for Cleveland Center for Contemporary Art.

1985-88 "Project for Well Fountain Park," commission for site-specific work in conjunction with the development of a new park in Brattleboro, Vermont.

1984 "Chapels of Ease," commission for Arts Festival of Atlanta, Georgia.

SELECTED GROUP EXHIBITIONS

1994 "The Language of Place," Riffe Gallery, Columbus, Ohio and The Museum of Modern Art, Saitama, Japan. Catalogue.

"Points of View," Retreti Art Center, Punkaharju, Finland. Catalogue.

1993 "The Robert J. Shiffler Collection," The Contemporary Art Center, Cincinnati, Ohio.

1992 "RSVP," Bechtler Gallery, Charlotte, North Carolina.

1991 "Mechanika," The Contemporary Arts Center, Cincinnati. Catalogue.

1990 "New Works for New Spaces: Into the Nineties," inaugural exhibition, part 3; Wexner Center for the Arts, Ohio State University, Columbus. Catalogue.

1990-91 "Awards in the Visual Arts," traveling to: New Orleans Museum of Art; Southeastern Center for Contemporary Art, Winston-Salem, North Carolina; Sackler Gallery, Cambridge, Massachusetts; BMW Gallery, New York.

1989 "Special Projects," P.S. 1 Museum, The Institute for Contemporary Art, Long Island City, New York.

1988-87 "Artists Choose Artists," Socrates Sculpture Park, Long Island City, New York.

1984 "Saying Good-bye to Grace," The Currier Gallery of Art, Manchester, New Hampshire.

1981 "Dream of Arcadia," Artpark, Lewiston, New York.

SELECTED GRANTS AND AWARDS

1995 Artist Fellowship, Ohio Arts Council.
(Also in 1991,1988).

1993 Project Grant, Art Matters, New York, for "The Difference between Religion and a Relationship with Christ."

1990-91 Awards in the Visual Arts 9, recipient, Southeastern Center for Contemporary Art.

1989 Artist Grant, Artists Space, New York.

1988 New Research Project Grant, College of The Arts, Ohio State University.

1987 Project Grant, The Athena Foundation, for "Scrapyard Temple for Socrates," Socrates Sculpture Park, Long Island City, New York.

SELECTED BIBLIOGRAPHY

Jacobson, Marjory. "Art for Work, The New Renaissance in Corporate Collecting." *Harvard Business School Press,* Cambridge, Massachusetts. (1993).

Sparks, Amy. "The Raven, Christ and the Body." *The Cleveland Free Times* (10 February 1993).

Sparks, Amy. Review of "New Works for New Spaces: Into the Nineties." *Dialogue* (January-February 1991).

Nesbitt, Lois E. Review of "New Works for New Spaces: Into the Nineties." *Columbia University Architecture, Planning, Preservation Journal.*

Vetrocq, Marcia E. "AVA 9." *Arts* (September 1990).

Carlock, Marty. "Waterfront Sites: Boston; 80s Boom, 90s Loom." *Public Art Review* (Winter/Spring 1989).

Trebay, Guy. "The Socratic Ideal." *The Village Voice* (7 June 1988).

Brenson, Michael. "Artists Choose Artists." *New York Times* (11 December 1987).

Zucker, Barbara. "Sculpture New Hampshire." *Art Journal* (Spring 1982).

WILLIE COLE

Born in Somerville, New Jersey, 1955.
Boston University School of Fine Arts, 1974-75.
BFA, The School of Visual Arts, New York, 1976.
The Arts Students League, New York 1976-79.

SELECTED INDIVIDUAL EXHIBITIONS

1995 "Our Daily Bread," The Fabric Workshop and Museum, Philadelphia.

1995 "The Elegba Principle," Capp Street Project, San Francisco.

1994 "Labor of Love," presented by The Contemporary at The Baltimore Museum of Industry. Brochure with text by Lisa G. Corrin.

Brooke Alexander, New York. (Also 1992).

1993 "Residue," Peter Miller Gallery, Chicago. (Also 1991).

1992 "Currents 51: Willie Cole," The Saint Louis Art Museum. Brochure with text by Charles Wylie.

1990 Special Projects, Institute For Contemporary Arts, P.S. 1, Long Island City, New York.

1986 "Dogs on Paper," Education Testing Service Corporation, Princeton, New Jersey.

SELECTED GROUP EXHIBITIONS

1995 "Promising Suspects," Aldrich Museum of Contemporary Art, Ridgefield, Connecticut.

1994 "re:visioning the familiar," Ezra and Cecile Zilkha Gallery, Wesleyan University, Middletown, Connecticut. Catalogue with text by Kenneth Miller and Tavern Pelletier.

"Other Visions: Composite," Neuberger Museum of Art, State University of New York at Purchase. Catalogue with text by Catherine Bernard.

"Old Glory: The American Flag in Contemporary Art," The Cleveland Center for Contemporary Art.

"Nor Here, Neither There," Los Angeles Contemporary Exhibitions, Los Angeles.

1993 "New Jersey Arts Annual," The Newark Museum, Newark, New Jersey.

"Dream Singers, Story Tellers: An African American Presence," New Jersey State Museum, Trenton; traveling to The Tokushima Modern Art Museum, Japan; Otani Memorial Art Museum; Fukui Fine Arts Museum, Fukui City, Japan. Catalogue.

1992 "Assemblage," Southeastern Center for Contemporary Art, Winston-Salem, North Carolina.

SELECTED GRANTS AND AWARDS

1995 Artist-in-residence, Capp Street Project, San Francisco.

1994 Wheeler Foundation Grant.

Artist-in-Residence, Pilchuck Glass School, Seattle.

Artist-in-Residence, The Contemporary, Baltimore.

1991 The Penny McCall Foundation Grant.

Rutgers Center for Innovative Printmaking Fellowship, Mason Gross School of the Arts, Rutgers University, New Brunswick, New Jersey.

1989 Artist-in-Residence, The Studio Museum in Harlem, New York.

SELECTED BIBLIOGRAPHY

Raynor, Vivan. "Piecing Together a Multicultural Heritage," *The New York Times* (7 August 1994).

Smith, Roberta. "Benefit Exhibition and Sale for Independent Curators." *The New York Times* (3 June 1994).

Upshaw, Reagan. "Willie Cole, Brooke Alexander." *Art in America* (May 1994).

Donaldson, Suzanne. "Willie Cole: Modern Brands." *Interview* (April 1992).

Heartney, Eleanor. "Willie Cole at Brooke Alexander." *Art in America* (5 May 1992).

Levin, Kim. "Willie Cole." *The Village Voice* (5 May 1992).

Yood James. "Willie Cole, Peter Miller Gallery." *Artforum* (January 1992).

Ziolkowski, Thad. "Willie Cole." *Artforum* (September 1992).

Sherlock, Maureen P. "Willie Cole." *Arts* (December 1990).

Appley, John. "Collective artwork is focus of 4+4 Exhibit." *The Plain Dealer* (October 26, 1990).

Cohen, Jean. "Is 90." *Sculpture* (September/October 1990).

SIMON GRENNAN & CHRISTOPHER SPERANDIO

Simon Grennan
Born in London, England, 1965.
Reading University, England, BA
University of Illinois at Chicago, MFA 1990.

Christopher Sperandio
Born in Kingwood West Virginia, 1964.
West Virginia University, Morgantown, BFA
University of Illinois at Chicago, MFA. 1991.

SELECTED INDIVIDUAL EXHIBITIONS

1995 Institute of Contemporary Art, London.

American Fine Arts Company, New York.

Cornerhouse, Manchester, England.

1994 "Recollections," Center for the Arts, Yerba Buena Gardens, San Francisco.

"Six Eastborne Dentists," Tower Gallery, Eastborne, England.

"Everyone in Farnham," James Hockney Gallery, Farnham, Surrey, England.

"Anyone in Britain," a project for *Telegraph Magazine,* London.

"Maintenance," Gahlberg Gallery, College of DuPage, Chicago.

1993 "Anyone in New York," Grey Art Gallery at New York University, New York.

"Lotus Club," Daniel Buchholz Gallery, Cologne, Germany.

1992 "At Home with the Collection," Lakeview Museum, Peoria, Illinois.

"Special Curation of the Astley Cheetham Collection," Manchester, England.

1991 "Sugar Additions at Civic Sites," Castlefield Gallery, Manchester, England.

Galerie der Stadt Fellbach, Stadt Museum Fellbach, Stuttgart, Germany.

Evanston Art Center, Evanston, Illinois.

1990 "The Body," (five simultaneous installations in five landmark churches), Chicago.

SELECTED GROUP EXHIBITIONS

1995 "Chocolate!" Swiss Institute, New York.

1994 American Fine Arts Co., New York.

1993 "Culture in Action," Sculpture Chicago, Chicago, Illinois.

Laure Genillars Gallery, London.

Anderson O'Day Gallery, London.

Jersey City Museum, New Jersey.

Andrea Rosen Gallery, New York.

1992 "Comfort ae Dissent," Artist Space, New York.

1991 "Profiles," Randolph Street Gallery, Chicago.

SELECTED PUBLICATIONS

"Recollections." Published by Center for the Arts, San Francisco, 1994.

"Six Eastborne Dentists." Published by Tower Gallery, Eastborne, England, 1994.

"Everyone in Farnham." Published by James Hockney Gallery, 1994.

SELECTED BIBLIOGRAPHY

Catalogue with text by Michael Benson, published by Bay Press, 1995.

Bulka, Michael F. "The Body: Various Churches." *New Art Examiner* (November 1990).

Cameron, Dan. "Culture in Action: eliminate the middleman." *Flash Art* (November 1993): 62-3.

Corrin, Lisa. "Mining The Museum: an Installation Confronting History," *The New Press* (December 1993): 302-13.

Heartney, Eleanor. "The Dematerialization of Public Art." *Sculpture Magazine* (March 1993).

Kimmelman, Michael. "Of Candy Bars and Public Art." *New York Times* (26 September 1993).

Princenthal, Nancy. "The New Realism: Everyone in Farnham." Catalogue. (July 1994).

Robinson, Walter. "A Taste for Public Art." *Art in America* (July 1993): 118.

Sales, Nancy. "Anyone in New York." *New York Magazine* (4 October 1993).

Tormollan, Carol. "Culture in Action."*High Performance* (Spring 1994): 50-53.

Yates, Robert. "Every One a Hero." *The Guardian* (7 April 1995).

CAROLYN HEALY

Born in Richland, Washington, 1950.
Swarthmore College, Swarthmore, Pennsylvania.
New School of Music, Philadelphia.

SELECTED INSTALLATION PROJECTS

1995 "Just as a Clasp Draws the Hair," site-specific installation for "Chance Encounters," Morris Gallery, Pennsylvania Academy of the Fine Arts, Museum of American Art, Philadelphia.

"No Time for Tears," site-specific installation for "A Closer Look," Beaver College Art Gallery, Glenside, Pennsylvania.

1994 "Canon in Six Parts," site-specific installation for "Objects and Souvenirs: Artists' Multiples," Rosenwald-Wolf Gallery, University of the Arts, Philadelphia.

1991 "Ether/Aura: An Electromagnetic Event," site specific installation (with John Phillips) for "Interactions," Institute of Contemporary Art, Philadelphia.

1990 "Shallow Breathing," site-specific installation (with sound by John Phillips), Hewlett Gallery, Carnegie-Mellon University, Pittsburgh.

1988 "Molly in Venice," sculptural environment and lighting (second version) with performance by Joanna Peled and sound by John Phillips, International James Joyce Symposium, Cini Foundation, Venice

1987 "Molly Bloom," sculptural environment and lighting (first version) with performance by Joanna Peled and sound by John Phillips, La Mama Theater, New York; The Temple Gallery, Philadelphia; Symphony Space, New York.

SELECTED EXHIBITIONS

1994 "Works on Paper," Beaver College Art Gallery. (Also in 1992)

1991 "Biennial '91," Delaware Art Museum, Wilmington.

1985 "Small Monuments," Temple Gallery, Philadelphia.

1981 "Dog Days Sculpture," Painted Bride Art Center, Philadelphia.

1980 "Recent Work," solo exhibition at Marian Locks Gallery, Philadelphia.

1979 "New Talent Show," Marian Locks Gallery.

"Artists of the Alliance," Philadelphia Art Alliance.

"Objects," solo show at Marian Locks Gallery.

SELECTED GRANTS AND AWARDS

1993 The Dietrich Foundation, Project Grant.

Pennsylvania Council on the Arts, Project Grant.

Pennsylvania Council on the Arts, Fellowship.

SELECTED BIBLIOGRAPHY

Kenton, Mary Jean. Review of "Shallow Breathing," *The New Art Examiner* (May 1989).

Rice, Robin. Review of "Ether/Aura," *City Paper* (23 June 1991).

Seidel, Miriam. Review of Ether/Aura,"(performance), *The Philadelphia Inquirer* (7 June 1991).

Sosanski, Edward. Review of "Ether/Aura," *The Philadelphia Inquirer* (2 June 1991).

HOMER JACKSON

Born in Philadelphia, Pennsylvania, 1957.
Philadelphia College of Art, Philadelphia, BFA, 1980.
Tyler School of Art, Philadelphia, MFA, 1982.

SELECTED EXHIBITIONS

1995 "Can't Trust A Big Butt and A Smile: Rethinking the Mami Wota Legend," Hallwalls Arts Center, Buffalo, New York.

"Can't Sweep: An Installation," Gutierrez Fine Arts Gallery, Miami Beach, Florida.

"Don't Smoke in Bed," Art in General, New York.

1994 "Women and Children First: Emergency Art from Behind Bars," Elizabeth Klein Gallery, Philadelphia.

1993 "High Flying," Institute of Contemporary Art, Philadelphia. Also Intermedia Arts, Minneapolis.

1992 "Speaking In Our Own Tongues," Taller Puertoriqueño, Philadelphia.

1991 "Philadelphia Art Now/Artists Choose Artists," Institute of Contemporary Art, Philadelphia. Catalogue with text by Julie Courtney.

1983 "SITES: 1982-85," Smithsonian Institute Traveling Exhibition, Washington DC.

"Opens Friday," Moore College of Art and Design, Philadelphia.

PERFORMANCES

1994 "Yacub: Mad Scientist or Genius," Arron Davis Hall, New York. Also Intermedia Arts, Minneapolis,1992.

1993 "Many Mansions," Delaware Center for the Contemporary Arts, Wilmington, Delaware.

1991 "Blues and the Naked Truth: Tales of Sex, Love, Lust and Sex," Painted Bride Art Center, Philadelphia.

"Empty Arms," Yellow Springs Institute, Chester Springs, Pennsylvania.

1990 "Affirmative Action: A Variety Show," Hallwalls Art Center, Buffalo, New York; The Wayspace, Miami, Florida.(Also Painted Bride Art Center and Movement Theater International, Philadelphia).

1984 "Searching for Charlie Parker," radio performance, WRTI FM, Philadelphia.

SELECTED GRANTS AND AWARDS

1995 Art Matters, Fellowship.

1994 Franklin Furnace, Fund for Performance Grant.

1993 Pennsylvania Council on the Arts,
Media Arts Fellowship.

1992 National Endowment for the Arts, Radio Fellowship.
(Also in 1991, 1989).

Pennsylvania Humanities Council, Project Grant for Radio.

1991 Pennsylvania Council on the Arts,
Interdisciplinary Grant. Also in 1990.

1990 Mid Atlantic Foundation/Pittsburgh
Filmmaker Fellowship.

1988 Pennsylvania Radio Theater, Radio Fellowship.
Also 1991.

National Endowment for the Arts/New Forms
Regrant Fellowship.

New American Radio, Radio Fellowship.

SELECTED BIBLIOGRAPHY

Mullinax, Gary. "Unconvential Performance Art."
The Wilmington News Journal (27 May 1993): D1, D2.

"Sneakers as Symbols of Black Male Power:
Self Interviews with Lloyd Lawrence and Homer Jackson."
Real News (15 March 1993):9-11.

Rice, Robin "Big Stuff: Words, Dresses and Basketball
Sneakers at the ICA."
Philadelphia City Paper (15 March 1993):15.

Rice, Robin "Outside In: The Language of Paper and
Messages From Behind Bars In Two Current Shows."
Philadelphia City Paper (11 February 1994):15.

Sinclair, Abiola "Media Watch: Yacub; Mad Scientist
or Genius?" *New York Amsterdam News*
(7 May 1994):26.

Campisi, Gloria. "Five Artist: Learning , Always Teaching."
The Philadelphia Daily News (3 February 1994):42-43.

RICHARD S. JORDAN

Born in Philadelphia, Pennsylvania.
Philadelphia College of Art, Philadelphia, 1974-76.
Pennsylvania Academy of Fine Arts, Philadelphia, 1976-78.
The Sculpture of Sem Ghelardini Pietrasanta, Italy, 1984-85.

SELECTED GROUP EXHIBITIONS

1995 "On the Corner," Painted Bride Art Center,
Philadelphia.

1993 Vermont Studio Center/ Philadelphia Fellows'
Exhibition, Philadelphia Art Alliance.

"High Flying," Institute of Contemporary Art,
University of Pennsylvania.

"Récherché 10th Anniversary/1983-1993," Sande Webster
Gallery, Philadelphia.

"Speaking In Our Tongues," Taller Puertorriqueño, Philadelphia.

1989 "Masks/Cultural and Contemporary," The Afro-
American Historical and Cultural Museum, Philadelphia.

"Noitallasmi/Installation," Moore College of Art and Design,
Philadelphia.

1987 "Den Flexible/Récherché Cultural Exchange,"
Charottenborg Museum, Copenhagen, Denmark. Catalogue.

1986 "Challenge Series," Fleisher Art Memorial, Philadelphia.

1984 "Art '84: Exhibition and Symposium," Aix-Les-Bains,
Palais Des Fleurs, France.

GRANTS AND AWARDS

1995-96 IPAP artists-in residence Award, Community
Education Center, Philadelphia.

1995 Pennsylvania Council on The Arts Award Fellowship in
Interdisciplinary Arts.

1992-93 Vermont Studio Center-Pew Award (Artist-in-
Residency), Johnson, Vermont.

CHRISTINA KUBISCH

Born in Bremen, Germany, 1948.
Academy of Fine Arts, Stuttgart, Germany, 1967-68.
The Academies of Music and Fine Arts in Hamburg,
Germany, and Graz, Austria, 1969-71.
Conservatory of Music and the Art School of Zurich
(Freie Kunstschule), Switzerland, 1972-74.
Conservatory Music, Milan, Italy. Graduated with Diploma,
1974-76.
The Technical Institute of Milan, 1980-81.

SELECTED INDIVIDUAL EXHIBITIONS

1994 Akademie der Kunst, Berlin.

Goethe House, London.

1993 De Vleeshal, Middleburg, Holland. Catalog.

Badisches Landesmuseum, Karlsruhe, Germany. Catalogue.

Museu de Arte Moderna, Belo Horizonte, Brazil. Catalogue.

Wellington City Art Gallery, Wellington, New Zealand.
Catalogue.

P3, Art and Enviroment, Tokyo. Catalogue.

1992 Neuer Berliner Kunstverein, Berlin. Catalogue.

1991 College of Art, Kyoto, Japan.

Musee Cantonal de Beaux Arts, Sion, Switzerland.
Catalogue.

Museum Fridericianum, Kassel, Germany.

1989 Walter Philips Gallery, Banff, Canada. Book.

SELECTED GROUP EXHIBITIONS

1995 "Sound and Art" The Ice Factory, Hannover, Germany.

1994 "Memento," Museum for Modern Art,
Prague, Czech Republic. .

Die Stillen, Sculpture Museum of Marl, Germany.

1993 "International Music Festival," Donaueschingen, Germany.

Achetas Space," Exoni Theater, Athens, Greece.

1991 "Artec," International Biennale of Nagoya, Japan.

"Umwandlungen," National Museum of Modern Art, Seoul,
Korea.

1990 "The 8th Biennial of Sydney," Art Gallery of New South
Wales, Sydney, Australia.

1987 "Documenta 8," Neue Galerie, Kassel, Germany.

1982 "Venice Bienale"

SELECTED GRANTS AND AWARDS

1995 DAAD Grant for Paris, France.

1994 Studio grant form the City of Berlin.

1991 Working grant from the City of Berlin.

1990 Project Grant from the Art Foundation, Bonn, Germany.

1986-89 Barkenhoff Residency, Worpswede, Germany.

1988 Award of the German Industrial Association (BDI).

SELECTED PUBLICATIONS

1993 "Interviews with Sound Artists," Het Apollohuis,
Eindhoven, Holland.

1994 "ERZAHLEN," Michael Glasmeyer, ed., Akademie der
Kunste, Berlin, Germany.

1995 "Christina Kubisch - Six Mirrors," Edition RZ, LC8846,
Berlin, Germany.

LLOYD LAWRENCE

Born in Philadelphia, Pennsylvania, 1957.
Tyler School of Art, Philadelphia, BFA, 1980.
University of Washington in Seattle, 1982-83.

SELECTED EXHIBITIONS

1995 "Don't Smoke in Bed," installation/collaboration with
artist Homer Jackson, Art in General, New York.

"Can't Trust a Big Butt and a Smile: Rethinking the Legend
of Mami Wota," installation and collaboration with artist
Homer Jackson, Hallwalls Contemporary Art Center,
Buffalo, New York.

1993 "High Flying," installation/collaboration with artist
Homer Jackson, Institute of Contemporary Art (ICA),
Philadelphia. (Also in 1994 as a part of the Essential Edge
program at Intermedia Art, Minneapolis.)

1990 "The Unportrait," Intermezzo Space, Osaka Japan.

1986 "WABI-SABI," Fuji Gallery, Kyoto, Japan.

1981 "New Drawings," Spoletto Art Festival, South Carolina (presented by Anewsawicz).

"The Underground, Philadelphia," Transitory Experimental Subway Space.

"Stolen Movements," Afro-American Historical and Cultural Museum, Philadelphia.

1980 "American in Rome Show," Oggi Gallery, Rome, Italy.

1977 "Emphasis," Baltimore Museum of Art, Baltimore, Maryland.

SELECTED PERFORMANCES

1995 "Communion: Issues of Contemporary Intimacy," Art in General, New York.

1994 Projects for the City Circus of "Rolywholyover: a Circus," a project of the Guggenheim Museum.

"Music for the Seen Seen and Heard Heard," The Center for Music Performance, New York University.

"Zero Sonata," Summer Stage Central Park, New York.

"Catching a Cereal Killer in Central Park," Summer Stage Central Park.

1991 "You," Great Wall, Beijing, People's Republic of China; Tan Park, Kyoung Jyu, Korea, and Ryoanji Zen Garden, Kyoto, Japan, performed during an armed student/government confrontation, tenth anniversary, Kyoung Jyu massacre.

1989 "Kamisama (Rice Man)," Hagiharatenjin, Japan.

1988 "Seeing Eye Dogs Believe in Zen," Fuji Gallery, Osaka, Japan.

1987 "Sin Eaters Anonymous," Hisaya Hotel, Osaka, Japan.

1986 "A Love/Death Chant for the Planet Earth," Eubie Blake Cultural Center, Baltimore.

"A Letter to Sharpville," The Occidental Loft, Seattle, Washington.

1985 "Atonal Drawing (For Muddy Waters)," Red Square, Seattle, Washington.

WINIFRED LUTZ

Born in Brooklyn, New York, 1942.
Cranbrook Academy of Art, MFA, 1968.
Cleveland Institute of Art, BFA, 1965.

SELECTED COMMISSIONS

1992-95 Permanent Outdoor Garden/Installation, The Mattress Factory, Pittsburgh, Pennsylvania.

1991 "Lifetime/Earthtime."A permanent outdoor stone garden, College of Wooster, Ohio.

1990 "How to Retain Site, Memory, While Developing the Landscape," Buttonwood Apartment Complex, Philadelphia.

SELECTED INDIVIDUAL EXHIBITIONS

1995 "Dome," site-integrated installation, The Contemporary Arts Center, Cincinatti, Ohio.

1992-95 "The Reclamation Garden," (evolving landscape project,) Abington Art Center, Pennsylvania. Brochure.

1991 "Mending Room," site-specific installation for "Artists Choose Artists," Institute of Contemporary Art, Philadelphia, Catalogue with text by Julie Courtney.

1990 "AGO\ANON," Grand Lobby installation, The Brooklyn Museum, Brooklyn, New York.

1987 "Ecco\Echo," Kunstcentrum Het Bassin, Maastrict, The Netherlands.

1986 "Light Cycle," performance, Visual Arts Center of Alaska, Anchorage, Alaska.

"A Point of View - A Vista," Hewlett Gallery, Carnegie Mellon University, Pittsburgh.

1984 "Counter Sanctuary/Viewfinder/Mediator," Fleisher Art Memorial, Philadelphia.

SELECTED GROUP EXHIBITIONS

1994 "USA With Limits," Galleria de Arte, Sao Paulo, Brazil.

1990 "A Natural Order, The Experience of the Landscape," The Hudson River Museum, Yonkers, New York.

1988 "The Cutting Edge," National Invitational, Kalamazoo Institute of Arts, Kalamazoo, Michigan. Catalogue with text by Charlotta Kotik

1988 "Correspondent Not Equivalent," part of "Paper Makes Space," International Paper Biennial Invitational, Leopold Hoesch Museum, Duren, Germany, and Nordjyllands Kuntmuseum, Aalborg, Denmark.

1987 "Tangents: Art in Fiber," Maryland Institute, College of Art, Baltimore, Maryland. Catalogue with text by Mary Jane Jacob.

"Craft Today: Poetry of the Physical," American Craft Museum, New York. Catalogue with text by Edward Lucie-Smith.

"Paper Now: Bent, Molded, Manipulated," international invitational, Cleveland Museum of Art, Cleveland Ohio. Catalogue with text by Jane Famer.

1983 "Paper As Image," International Invitational, Arts Council of Great Britain, London.

1982 "Cranbrook USA," Invitational, Cranbrook Academy of Art, Bloomfield Hills, Michigan

1980 "With Paper, About Paper," Albright-Knox Art Gallery, Buffalo, New York. Catalogue with text by Charlotta Kotik.

1978 "Paper as Medium," Smithsonian Institute Traveling Exhibition Service, Washington DC. Catalogue edited by Jane Famer.

SELECTED GRANTS AND AWARDS

1992 Pew Fellowship in the Arts.

1990 Frances J. Greenburger Foundation Award, New York City.

1990 Pennsylvania Council on the Arts, Visual Arts Fellowship.

1989 Creative Time, Inc. Project Grant.

1984 National Endowment for the Arts, Fellowship in Sculpture.

SELECTED BIBLIOGRAPHY

Abercrombie, Stanley "Winifred Lutz." FAIA. *Interior Design* (September 1992).

Campbell, Lawrence "Winifred Lutz at Marilyn Pearl and The Brooklyn Museum." *Art in America* (April 1991).

Gruen, Peter. "Viewpoint." *Dialogue: An Art Journal* (November\December 1986).

King, A. Elaine. *Sculpture Magazine* (January/February 1990).

Handy, Ellen. "10th Anniversary Exhibition."*Art Magazine* (December 1986).

Malarcher, Patricia. "Forceful Sculpture Arises from Paper." *The New York Times* (16 October 1988).

New York In Review. *Arts Magazine* (October 1990).

Russell, John. *The New York Times* (29 January 1988).

Bloomfield, Maureen. "Nuances of Numbers." *Dialogue: An Art Journal* (November-December 1986).

Feinberg, Jean. "Finding of Winifred Lutz." *Craft Horizons* (April 1979).

MOGAUWANE MAHLOELE

Born in Storomo, South Africa.

SELECTED EXHIBITIONS

1993 American Friends Center, Philadelphia.

1992 "Children of the Future," Brooklyn Museum, New York.

1991 First District Plaza, Philadelphia.

1990 Lincoln University, Philadelphia.

1988 Indingilizi Art Gallery, Swaziland.

1987 "International Trade Fair," Manzini, Swaziland. Also 1986 and 1985.

"Africa Day," Kwaluseni University, Swaziland. Also 1986, 1985, 1984, 1983.

1986 "Hhondo Sculptures," Harare, Zimbabwe.

1984 "Open Air," Gaberone, Botswana.

SELECTED PERFORMANCES

1995 Pennsylvania Prisons (various). (Also in 1994, 1993, 1992.)

1994 Temple of Maat, Wilmington, Delaware. (Also in 1993, 1992.)

Mellon Jazz Festival, Philadelphia.

1983 "Street Festival," Brooklyn, New York. (Also in 1992.)

1992 Knitting Factory, New York.

1991 Tvoune Stop Jazz Festival, Philadelphia.

1988 American Black Renaissance, Swaziland.

1987 Zila Greyhound Festival, Swaziland.

International Trade Fair, Mazini, Swaziland.
(Also 1986 and 1985.)

1985 Brixton Jazz Festival, London.

SELECTED THEATRICAL PERFORMANCES, MUSICAL COMPOSITION, AND CHOREOGRAPHY

1995 "Birth of a Drum," Philadelphia.

1987 "Oh Write My Name," Black Renaissance, Swaziland.

1983 "Born In R.S.A.," Philadelphia.

1984 "July's People," Philadelphia.

1980 "Chain Reaction," Swaziland.

VIRGIL MARTI

Born in St. Louis, Missouri, 1962.
Skowhegan School of Painting and Sculpture, Skowhegan, Maine, Summer 1990.
Tyler School of Art, Temple University, Philadelphia, MFA, 1990.
School of Fine Arts, Washington University, BFA, 1984.

SELECTED EXHIBITIONS

1994 "Fleisher Challenge #3," Samuel S. Fleisher Art Memorial, Philadelphia.

"Les Objets D`Artiste," Marian Locks Gallery, Philadelphia.

"Works On Paper 1994," Beaver College Art Gallery, Glenside, Pennsylvania. (Also 1992.)

"14 at 55," 55 Mercer, New York.

1993 "A Few Fey Things," White Columns, New York.

1992 "Energy Made Visible," Larry Becker, Philadelphia.

"Bully Wallpaper," Paley Gallery, Moore College of Art and Design, Philadelphia.

1991 "Biennial '91," Delaware Art Museum, Wilmington.

1990 "Virgil Marti and Stuart Netsky," The Temple Gallery, Philadelphia.

SELECTED GRANTS AND AWARDS

1995 Pew Fellowship in the Arts.

1995 Art Matters Fellowship.

1994 Philadelphia Museum of Art Purchase Award.

1992 Friends of Beaver College Art Gallery Award.

JOHN PHILLIPS

Born in Williamsport, Pennsylvania, 1950.
Boston University, 1967-69.
Pennsylvania Academy of the Fine Arts, 1969-73.

SELECTED PERFORMANCES AND INSTALLATIONS

1995 "E.G.A.C." for "Chance Encounters," Morris Gallery, Pennsylvania Academy of the Fine Arts, Museum of American Art, Philadelphia.

"Elegy for John S.," audio tape presented at the national conference of the Society of Electro Acoustic Music in the United States (SEAMUS), Ithaca College, Ithaca, New York.

1991 "Ether/Aura: An Electromagnetic Event," sound/light environment (with Carolyn Healy) for "Interactions," Institute of Contemporary Art, Philadelphia.

1990 "The things one has to listen to ..." and "Altitudes," tape works commissioned by New American Radio.

1989 "Shallow Breathing," sound/light environment (with Carolyn Healy), Hewlett Gallery, Carnegie-Mellon University, Pittsburgh.

"Nick's Dream," sound/light environment for Alice Forner & Dancers, Merce Cunningham Studio, New York.

1988 "Molly in Venice," sound/light environment (second version) with performance by Joanna Peled and set by Carolyn Healy, International James Joyce Symposium, Cini Foundation, Venice

"One night Stand #8," Merce Cunningham Studio, New York.

1987 "Molly Bloom," sound/light environment (first version) with performance by Joanna Peled and set by Carolyn Healy, La Mama Theater, New York; The Temple Gallery, Philadelphia.

"Lives Over Time," for Alice Forner Dance Co., Douglas Dunn Studio, New York.

GRANTS AND AWARDS

1995 National Endowment for the Arts, Artist Fellowship.

Pennsylvania Council on the Arts, Artist Fellowship (Also 1991).

1993 Pennsylvania Council on the Arts (with Carolyn Healy) (Also 1989).

1990 New Forms Regional Grant.

BIBLIOGRAPHY

Kenton, Mary Jean. Review of "Shallow Breathing," *The New Art Examiner* (May 1989).

Rice, Robin. Review of "Ether/Aura," *City Paper* (23 June 1991).

Seidel, Miriam. Review of "Ether/Aura," (performance), *The Philadelphia Inquirer* (7 June 1991).

Sosanski, Edward. Review of "Ether/Aura," (sculpture) *The Philadelphia Inquirer* (2 June 1991).

BRUCE POLLOCK

Born in Painesville, Ohio 1951.
Carnegie-Mellon University, Pittsburgh, Pennsylvania, 1970-71.
Cleveland Institute of Art, Cleveland, Ohio, BFA, 1976.
Temple University Abroad, Rome, 1976-77.
Tyler School of Art, Philadelphia, MFA, 1978.

SELECTED INDIVIDUAL EXHIBITIONS

1994 Philadelphia Art Alliance

1991 Janet Fleisher Gallery, Philadelphia. (Also 1989, 1987).

1990 "Thresholds." Morris Gallery, Pennsylvania Academy of Fine Art, Philadelphia.

"Polychrome Sculpture 1982-85." Design Arts Gallery, Nesbitt College of Design Arts, Drexel University, Philadelphia.

1986 Cavin Morris Gallery, New York.

1984 Lawrence Miller Gallery, New York.

1983 "Ariel," Florence Wilcox Gallery, Swarthmore, Pennsylvania.

1982 Allen Stone Gallery, New York.

Jeffrey Fuller Fine Art, Philadelphia.

1981 Dome Room Gallery, New Educational Center For the Arts., New Haven, Connecticut.

1979 Challenge Exhibition, Fleisher Art Memorial, Philadelphia.

SELECTED GROUP EXHIBITIONS

1994 "Concerning the Spiritual in Art," Chester Springs Studio, Yellow Springs, Pennsylvania.

"15 at 55," 55 Mercer Street, New York.

1993 "Ritual and Response: Abstract Painting," Hicks Art Center, Bucks County Community College, Newtown, Pennsylvania.

"Cybernetics in the Art of Learning: Meta This and Meta That," University of the Arts, Philadelphia.

1992 "On the Moon: Art In Science IX," (with Richard Torchia), Esther M. Klein Gallery, University City Science Center, Philadelphia.

1990 "Contemporary Philadelphia Artists," Philadelphia Museum of Art, Philadelphia.

1988 "Perspective On Pennsylvania," Carnegie-Mellon University Gallery, Pittsburgh, Pennsylvania.

1987 "Made in Philadelphia 7," Institute of Contemporary Art, Philadelphia.

"International," Stux Gallery, New York.

"Neo Alchemy," Cavin Morris Gallery, New York.

1979 "Summer," Morris Gallery, Pennsylvania Academy of Fine Arts, Philadelphia.

SELECTED GRANTS AND AWARDS

1989 Pollock-Krasner Foundation Grant.

1987 McDowell Colony Fellowship, Peterborough, New Hampshire.

1983 Pennsylvania Council On the Arts, Artist Fellowship.

SELECTED BIBLIOGRAPHY

Flood, Richard. "The Morris Gallery." *Artforum.*
(October 1977).

Holbrook, Johanna. "Ritual and Response: Abstract Painting
1993." *New Art Examiner.* (Vol. 21, NO. 4, 1993).

Jarmusch, Anne. "Vermeer in Philadelphia." *Artnews*
(March 1981):156.

Rice, Robin. "Spirit and Manflesh." *City Paper* (4 March 1994).

Rice, Robin. "Bruce Pollock and Richard Torchia."
New Art Examiner (May 1992): 40.

Sachs, Sid. "Bruce Pollock at Jeffrey Fuller."
New Art Examiner (October 1982).

Stein, Judith. "Bruce Pollock." *Art in America*
(October 1982): 70.

Sozanski, Edward. "In Search of Contemporary Art."
The Philadelphia Inquirer (13 March 1994).

Sozanski, Edward. "Art Alliance." *The Philadelphia Inquirer*
(18 March 1994).

Sozanski, Edward. "Bruce Pollock at Janet Fleisher."
The Philadelphia Inquirer (24 October 1991).

FIONA TEMPLETON

Born in North Lanarkshire, Scotland, 1951.
Edinburgh University, Edinburgh, Scotland, MA, 1973.
New York University, New York, MA, 1985.
Aix-en-Provence, France, 1971-72.

SELECTED WORKS AND COLLABORATIONS

1994 "Recognition," solo performance, National Review of
Live Art, Glasgow, Scotland.

1992 "Realities/Metamorphosis," Brooklyn Bridge
Anchorage, part of "The Spatial Drive," New Museum,
New York.

"Articulate Architecture," installation and workshops, Capp
Street Project, San Francisco. With Siobhan Liddel and
Robert Kocik.

1991 *"Delire d'Interpretations,"* commissioned play, Theatre
Cocteau, Basel, Switzerland.

1990 "Where on Earth," collaboration for Franklin Furnace
with five performers, New York.

"Du - Die Stadt," German version of "You - The City,"
Freispiel/Beck Forum, Munich (Also At Zurich Theater,
Spektakel, Den Haag, Holland and Ljubljana, Yugoslavia.)

1989 "You - The City," London International
Festival of Theater.

1988 "You - The City," New York.

1980 "Thought/Death," solo performance at Acme Gallery,
London. (Also Annina Nosei Gallery and Whitney Museum of
American Art, New York; Polyphonix Festival, Paris; 80 Langton
Street, San Francisco; Paul Steen Gallery, Edinburgh.)

1974-79 Director, cofounder, Theater of Mistakes, London.

SELECTED GRANTS AND AWARDS

1995 National Endowment for the Arts, Artist
Fellowship, Poetry.

1994 Art Matters Grant (Also in 1988).

1989 New York Foundation for Arts Performance Fellowship
(Also in 1985).

New York State Council on the Arts project Grant
(Also 1987).

1987 Foundation for Contemporary Performance Arts Grant.

1986 PEN Writers' Fund Grant.

National Endowment for the Arts, Interarts Project Grant.

1983 National Endowment for the Arts, Artists Fellowship,
New Genres.

PUBLICATIONS

Delerium of Interpretations, Sun and Moon Press,
Los Angeles, 1995.

"You - the City," film produced by Fiona Templeton, 1995.

Hi, Cowboy, Pointing Device, London, 1995.

You - The City, Segue, New York, 1990; Dutch version,
JIJ - De Staat, published by Het Gebeuren, Den Haag, 1991.

London, Sun & Moon Press, College Park, Maryland, 1984.

Elements of Performance Art, with Anthony Howell, Ting Books,
London, 1986.

ALLEN WEXLER

Born in Bridgeport, Connecticut, 1949.
Pratt Institute, Master of Architecture, 1976.
Rhode Island School of Design, Bachelor of Architecture, 1971.
Rhode Island School of Design, Bachelor of Fine Arts, 1971.

SELECTED INDIVIDUAL EXHIBITIONS

1994 Ronald Feldman Fine Art, New York.
(Also 1992, 1990, 1988, 1985.)

"The Small Buildings, Furniture and Utensils of Allen Wexler,"
Hochschule der Kunste, Berlin, Germany.

1993 "Allen Wexler - Structures for Reflection," Karl Ernst
Osthaus Museum, Hagen, Germany. Traveled to Kunstverein
Braunschweig, Germany; Galerie Am Fischmarkt, Erfurt;
Germany; Wilhelm Hack Museum, Ludwigshafen; Museum
Voor Sierkunst, Ghent, Belgium. Catalogue with text by
Michael Fehr and Kim Levin.

1992 "Table/Building/Landscape and Proposals for a Picnic
Area," De Cordova Museum and Sculpture Park,
Lincoln, Massachusetts.

1991 "Table/Building/Landscape," The Forum Gallery,
St. Louis, Missouri.

"Allen Wexler," San Diego Museum of Contemporary Art,
La Jolla, California.

1989 "Allen Wexler: Dining Rooms and Furniture for the
Typical House," University Gallery, University of
Massachusetts at Amherst. Catalogue text Betsy Siersma.

"Allen Wexler," Institute of Contemporary Art, University of
Pennsylvania. Catalogue with text by Judith Tannenbaum.

1988 "Sukkah Installation," The Jewish Museum, New York.

1986 The Temple Gallery, Philadelphia.

1985 Brown University, List Art Center, Providence, Rhode Island.

SELECTED GROUP EXHIBITIONS

1994 "House Rules," The Wexner Center for the Arts,
The Ohio State University, Columbus.

1993 "Discursive Dress," John Michael Kohler Arts Center,
Sheboygan, Wisconsin.

"Construction in Process IV: My Home is Your Home," The Artists'
Museum, Tylana, Poland and The Artists' Museum, New York.

1991 "Construction of Meanings," University Galleries,
Illinois State University, Normal. Catalogue.

1990 "Sukkah Built from Furniture Walls," Israel Museum,
Jerusalem.

1988 "Bed/Sitting Room for Artists in Residence,"
permanent installation, Mattress Factory Gallery, Pittsburgh,
Pennsylvania. Catalogue.

1987 "Pure Room for the Memory Theater of Giulio Camillo,"
Neuberger Museum, SUNY at Purchase, New York.

1986 "Pure Room for the Memory Theater of Giulio Camillo,"
installation collaboration at the Brooklyn Bridge Anchorage,
New York.

SELECTED GRANTS AND AWARDS

1990 New York Foundation for the Arts, Fellowship Award.
(Also 1985.)

1989 New York State Council on the Arts, Sponsored
Project Award.

1986 Bessie Award, for stage set of "Memory Theater."

SELECTED BIBLIOGRAPHY

Seward, Keith. "Allen Wexler." *Artforum* (February 1995): 90.

Levin, Kim. "Voices Choices." *The Village Voice*
(13 December 1994): 10.

Fehr, Michael. "Allen Wexler, Crate House." *Domus Magazine*
(October 1993): 20-23

Phillips, Patricia. "Sitting Up: Critical Chairs." *Sculpture
Magazine* (Summer 1993) :24-31.

Cembalest, Robin. "Reviews." *Artnews* (April 1992): 121.

Cotter, Holland. "Allen Wexler - On the Dubious Comforts of
Home." *The New York Times* (31 January 1992): C 19.

Heartney, Eleanor. "Review of Exhibitions." *Art in America*
(June 1992): 103.

Koplos, Janet. "Allen Wexler at Ronald Feldman."
Art in America (June 1990): 181-82.

Neff, Eileen. *Artforum* (September 1989).

Princenthal, Nancy. "After Tilted Arch at Storefront for Art
and Architecture." *Art in America* (February 1987).

"Wexler at McIntosh/Drysdale." *The Washington Post*
(20 December 1987).